WITHDRAWN

D1540333

TWAYNE'S WORLD AUTHORS SERIES

A Survey of the World's Literature

Sylvia E. Bowman, Indiana University

GENERAL EDITOR

FRANCE

Maxwell A. Smith, Guerry Professor of French, Emeritus
The University of Chattanooga
Former Visiting Professor in Modern Languages
The Florida State University

EDITOR

Pierre de Ronsard

(TWAS 132)

TWAYNE'S WORLD AUTHORS SERIES (TWAS)

The purpose of TWAS is to survey the major writers—novelists, dramatists, historians, poets, philosophers, and critics—of the nations of the world. Among the national literatures covered are those of Australia, Canada, China, Eastern Europe, France, Germany, Greece, India, Italy, Japan, Latin America, New Zealand, Poland, Russia, Scandinavia, Spain, and the African nations, as well as Hebrew, Yiddish, and Latin Classical literatures. This survey is complemented by Twayne's United States Authors Series and English Authors Series.

The intent of each volume in these series is to present a critical-analytical study of the works of the writer; to include biographical and historical material that may be necessary for understanding, appreciation, and critical appraisal of the writer; and to present all material in clear, concise English—but not to vitiate the scholarly content of the work by doing so.

Pierre de Ronsard

By K. R. W. Jones

University of the South

Twayne Publishers, Inc.   ::   New York

St. Mary's College Library

841
R669
J719

Copyright © 1970 by Twayne Publishers, Inc.
All Rights Reserved

Library of Congress Catalog Card Number: 75-120502

MANUFACTURED IN THE UNITED STATES OF AMERICA

Preface

In keeping with the purpose of this series, I have attempted to present an introduction to the principal collections of the poetry of Pierre de Ronsard. In doing so I have also endeavored to place the poems in perspective by mentioning something of the intellectual, artistic, and social movements of the French Renaissance which contributed so richly to the poet's formation and maturity.

Little attempt has been made to deal with certain stylistic problems which a more detailed examination of Ronsard's poetry would certainly raise. A discussion of such complex problems as the relation of certain works to the mannerist or baroque styles seemed better omitted in view of the introductory nature of the present study. I have likewise refrained from attempting a superficial survey of the posthumous fortunes óf Ronsard's poetry and its influence in France.

The selection of poems studied in some detail may seem purely arbitrary, though in many instances the choice has been made with the purpose of avoiding the repetition of the short lyric works and sonnets which appear in almost every available anthology or general introduction. By selecting poems which, though less well known, are equally typical I have hoped to indicate something of the variety and scope of the poet's achievement not usually apparent to those familiar with only a few poems.

For the translations I offer no apology. They have little to recommend them but clarity and fidelity to the French text, to which they are meant simply as an introduction and guide.

To acknowledge the debts I owe to scholars past and present would be impossible; the notes and bibliography give some indication, but many works both general and specialized have of necessity been omitted. This omission does not imply oversight or ingratitude but is dictated by the limits of this study. One debt, however, can not be passed in silence. I wish to express particular thanks to Professor Isidore Silver, not only for the many contributions to Ronsard studies which

35197

have helped the present work, but also for his kind and generous encouragement during the course of his seminar on Ronsard at the Southeastern Medieval and Renaissance Institute.

Finally I should like to thank my colleagues of the University of the South for their encouragement and advice, Mrs. T. Stovall for her care in typing the manuscript, and Professor Maxwell Smith and the editors of the Twayne Series.

K. R. W. J.

Sewanee, Tennessee
September, 1968

Contents

Chronology

1469   Birth of Louis de Ronsart, father of the poet, at the château of La Possonnière near Couture, Vendômois.

1494-   Louis de Ronsart engaged in the Italian wars.
1515

1500   Louis de Ronsart made knight (*chevalier*) by Louis XII.

1515   (February 2) Marriage of Louis de Ronsart and Jeanne de Chaudrier.

1518   Louis de Ronsart named *maistre d'hostel* to the dauphin.

1524   (September 10-11) Birth of Pierre de Ronsard at the château of La Possonnière.

1526   Louis de Ronsart accompanies the two sons of François I to Madrid, where they remain for four years as hostages for their father after his capture by Imperial troops at the Battle of Pavia.

1533-   Ronsard spends a term at the Collège de Navarre in Paris.
1534   Withdrawn because of unsatisfactory studies.

1535   Inherits the rather good library of his uncle, curé of Bessé-sur-Braye (perhaps one of his early tutors).

1536   (August) Placed as page at the French court. Witnesses the sudden death and autopsy of his first master, François, eldest son of the king. Enters the service of Charles, Duc d'Orléans, third son of François I. Follows court during festivities for the wedding of Madeleine de France and James V of Scotland.

1537   Witnesses the wedding of Madeleine de France and James V in Notre-Dame-de-Paris. (Spring) Ronsard, now a page in the household of Madeleine, sails to Scotland. (August) After the death of Madeleine, returns with her household to France.

1538-   (December 24-March 24) With the French envoy Ronsard
1539   returns to Scotland by way of Flanders. The ship is nearly lost at sea off the coast of Scotland. In Edinburgh he may have met an Italian nobleman "le seigneur Paul" who introduced him to Latin poets. Returns through England.

1539   Ronsard, no longer a page, enters the Royal Riding School in Paris, an academy for the sons of noblemen. Reads Latin poetry with "seigneur Paul."

1540 (May-August) In the suite of Lazare de Baïf, humanist and diplomat, Ronsard attends a conference of French and German churchmen and scholars at Haguenau, Alsace.

1540-
1543 After a severe fever, Ronsard remains partly deaf. Recuperates at the family estate at La Possonnière, reading poetry and composing first odes. Father urges him to follow a career in law.

1543 (March 5-6) With his father Ronsard attends the funeral of Guillaume de Langey du Bellay in the cathedral of Le Mans. Receives simple tonsure from the bishop of Le Mans, René du Bellay. While there he shows his poems to the bishop's secretary, Jacques Peletier du Mans, who encourages his efforts.

1544 (June 6) Death of Louis de Ronsart. Ronsard goes to Paris to resume his studies.

1544-
1547 Studies Greek and Latin with the son of Lazare de Baïf, Jean-Antoine, under the direction of Jean Dorat.

1545 (April 21) At a court ball in Blois, sees Cassandre Salviati, daughter of a wealthy Florentine banker. Death of Ronsard's mother.

1546 Marriage of Cassandre Salviati and the Seigneur de Pray, a neighbor of the Ronsards. Ronsard composes his first Pindaric odes.

1547 Jacques Peletier publishes his *O'Euvres Poëtiques,* containing Ronsard's first published ode. Jean Dorat named principal of the Collège de Coqueret at Paris. Joachim du Bellay meets Ronsard at an inn(?). Together with Jean-Antoine de Baïf they enter the Collège de Coqueret to study under Dorat.

1549 Ronsard publishes several poems celebrating the royal family. Du Bellay, encouraged and assisted by Ronsard, publishes *La Deffence et Illustration de la Langue Françoyse.* (Summer) Coqueret students make an excursion to the village of Arcueil near Paris for a humanist picnic.

1550 Publication of Ronsard's *Quatre Premiers Livres des Odes* and his first *Bocage.* (May or June) Mellin de Saint-Gelais makes a sly attack on the *Odes* before the court of Henri II at the Louvre. Ronsard is defended by Marguerite de France, the king's sister, and her chancellor, Michel de L'Hospital. Ronsard composes odes for them.

1551 Contributes a poem for the *Tombeau de Marguerite de Navarre.*

1551-
1553 At the Collège de Boncourt in Paris future members of the "brigade" study under Galland and the humanist Marc-Antoine de Muret: Belleau, La Peruse, Jodelle, and Grevin.

1552 Publication of *Le Premier Livre des Amours.*

1553   Following two successful performances of Jodelle's tragedy *Cleopastre Captive,* students of Coqueret and Boncourt celebrate at Arcueil with a banquet. (March) Second edition of *Odes.* Publication (anonymous) of the *Livret de Folastries.* (May) Second edition of *Amours* with a commentary by Muret. (August) Augmented edition of *Odes.* During the autumn Ronsard seeks refuge from the plague first at his benefice near Meaux, then in the Vendômois.

1554   From the judges of the Jeux Floraux in Toulouse, Ronsard receives the prize of the Eglantine, later made into a silver statuette of Minerva and presented to Henri II. He is called by the judges *Poëte du Roy.* Ronsard begins the *Franciade* but soon lays it aside.

1555   Publication of *Meslanges* and third edition of *Odes.* Ronsard meets Marie at Bourgueil in Anjou. (August) Publication of *Continuation des Amours.* (November) Publication of the first book of *Hymnes.* Obtains an ecclesiastical appointment at Evaillé in Maine.

1556   Publication of the *Nouvelle Continuation des Amours* and the second book of *Hymnes.*

1557   Reprinting of the two *Continuations.* Ronsard makes efforts to obtain ecclesiastical preferments with help of members of the Chastillon and Guise families, but to no avail.

1558-   Publishes several poems celebrating war, peace, and marriages
1559   of the royal family. *Sonets à Sinope,* whose identity remains a mystery. Ronsard is named *aumosnier ordinnaire du Roy* and *conseiller du Roy.*

1560   Death of Joachim du Bellay. (April) Ronsard and Baïf visit in Touraine and Anjou, where they attend a country wedding. Preface for *Meslanges et chansons* dedicated to François II. (December) Publication of first collected edition of Ronsard's *OEuvres.* Ronsard named canon of the cathedral church of St.-Julien at Le Mans.

1561   Beginning of one-year affair with Genèvre in Paris. Her identity still the subject of speculation. (September) Ronsard attends the Colloquy of Poissy between Catholics and Protestants. Its failure is soon followed by outbreaks of civil strife.

1562-   Ronsard, at the head of armed men, defends his property in Maine against Protestant marauders. Publication of the *Institution pour l'Adolescence du Roy Charles IX* and the two *Discours sur les Misères de ce temps.*

1562-   Protestant writers attack Ronsard in pamphlets and poems.
1563   Publication of *Remonstrance au Peuple de France* and *Response aux injures et calomnies de ie ne sçay quels*

Ministres de Genève. (October) Publication of *Recueil des Nouvelles Poësies* containing *Hymnes des IIII [sic] Saisons.* Sonnets for Isabeau de Limeuil. Disappointed by failure to receive remuneration for his poems for the court, Ronsard publishes *La Promesse,* dedicated to the Queen Mother, Catherine de Medici.

1564   For royal celebrations at Fontainebleau and Bar-le-Duc, Ronsard composes cartels, mascarades, and a dramatic pastoral, *La Bergerie;* all these are published the following year.

1565   (March) Ronsard is named prior of Saint-Cosme-lez-Tours. (April) For the celebrations of the royal family at Bayonne Ronsard composes poems sent from Bordeaux, where he is a guest of Belot. (July) Publications of *Elegies, Mascarades et Bergerie.* (November) Receives Charles IX and the Queen Mother at Saint-Cosme. Receives the order to begin work again on the *Franciade.* Anonymous publication of the *Abrégé de l'Art Poëtique françois.*

1566   Ronsard exchanges the benefice at Evaillé for a prebendary at the collegiate church of Saint-Martin at Tours. Receives from his secretary the priory of Croixval in Vendômois. During part of the year Ronsard is in Paris suffering from a fever.

1567   Attends a performance of Baïf's comedy *Le Brave* at the Hôtel de Guise. (April) Second collected edition of the *OEuvres.* (September) Sits on a jury to examine a candidate for the chair of Greek in the Collège Royal (now the Collège de France). Follows the court to Meaux and then back to Paris. Two fragments of the *Franciade* in Alexandrine verse are published in Denis Lambin's edition of Horace.

1568   Most of the year is spent in rural retreat at Croixval and Saint-Cosme with Amadys Jamyn. Ronsard suffers from quartan fever.

1569   Celebrates in several poems the victories of the royal armies over the Protestants. (August) Publication of the *VIe et VIIe Livres des Poëmes.*

1570   Composition of *Eurymedon et Callirée* for Charles IX. After the Peace of Saint-Germain, Ronsard returns to court where he may have met for the first time Hélène de Surgères, lady-in-waiting to the Queen Mother. He composes on commission the *Sonets et Madrigaux pour Astrée.*

1571   With Dorat, Ronsard contributes poems and mottoes for the festivities in honor of Charles IX and his new queen, Elizabeth of Austria. Book IV of the *Franciade* read before the king at Blois. At court Ronsard meets Tasso and Orlando di Lasso. Publication of third collected edition of the *OEuvres.*

1572   Begins the *Sonets pour Helene* for Hélène de Surgères. Preface for a collection of poems set to music. (September) Publication of the first four books of the *Franciade*.

1573   Fourth collected edition of the *OEuvres*. Ronsard asked to contribute poems for the court reception of the Polish ambassadors.

1574   Publication of the *Tombeau de Charles IX*. Poems for the accession of Henri III. On the death of Marie de Clèves, mistress of the new king, Ronsard composes poems *Sur la Mort de Marie*.

1575   Publication of the *Tombeau de Marguerite de France*. Spends winter at Croixval.

1576   Most of the year spent at Croixval and Saint-Cosme. With Desportes and Jamyn, Ronsard attends the funeral of Belleau in Paris.

1577   Many of Ronsard's poems set to music and published in anthologies. Attends the court festivals at châteaux in Touraine.

1578   Fifth collected edition of *OEuvres*. This edition contains the first printing of the *Sonets pour Helene*.

1579   Long stay at priory of Saint-Cosme.

1581   Ronsard joins in contributing poems for the celebrations of the marriage of the Duc de Joyeuse, a royal favorite. (November) Returns from court to Saint-Cosme.

1583   Spends much of the year at Croixval and Saint-Cosme. Because of illness he is unable to represent the chapter of St.-Martin-de-Tours at the provincial synod. On returning to Paris he is the guest of Galland, principal of the Collège de Boncourt.

1584   Publication of the sixth collected edition of the *OEuvres* in folio, containing the *Bocage royal*. After seeing this edition through the press, he returns to Croixval in the spring.

1585   Ronsard's last stay in Paris. He is suffering from his last sickness. (June) On a specially constructed litter he returns to Croixval by way of Saint-Gilles de Montoire. (December) Driven out by roaming bands of Protestant troops, Ronsard leaves Croixval for a painful flight to Saint-Cosme. After dictating his will and last poems to Galland he dies on the night of December 27-28 and is buried in the choir of the priory church.

1586   (February 24) Elaborate memorial service for Ronsard at the Collège de Boncourt: requiem mass, composed by Jacques Mauduit, sung by musicians of the Chapel Royal with instruments from the King's Academy, followed by banquet in the refectory and orations. Many from the court and university attend. Honor guests are presented the first edition of Ronsard's *Derniers Vers.* Claude Binet publishes the first version of his *Vie de Ronsard.* Two other versions will follow. Two *Tombeaux,* one in Latin, the other in French, honor the memory of Ronsard. Desportes is notable by his absence.

1587   Posthumous edition of collected *OEuvres* under supervision of Binet and Galland. Eight other editions, closely resembling this, appear: 1592; 1597; 1604; 1609 (two); 1617; 1629; and 1630, the last edition till the nineteenth century.

CHAPTER 1

Introduction

E VER since the Romantics began to rescue the works of Ronsard
from the oblivion into which they had fallen for almost two
centuries, the public has been faced with a succession of studies seeking
to restore to the Prince of Poets some of the luster he enjoyed during
his own lifetime. Biographers have devoted their labors to disinterring
the details of his life, his ancestors and family, his friends and enemies.
Others have endeavored to make Ronsard's poetry more comprehen-
sible in the light of the events of his times, events in which he was
frequently directly concerned. Philologists and editors, aided by early
commentators, have gradually put together an imposing array of
literary sources, ancient and modern, upon which Ronsard may or may
not have drawn in the composition of his work. Most recently, changes
in critical methods have called into question the relevance of older
scholarship and focused attention on structure, theme, and tone, and
on the connections between the poetry of Ronsard and the intellectual
and artistic movements of the Renaissance.

For all these endeavors the lover of Ronsard's poetry must indeed be
grateful. And yet one has the decided impression that many of the
labors of scholarship have made but slight impression on the public
which is cognizant of French letters. True, the reputation of Ronsard as
one of the greatest poets in the language is now firmly established; but
this reputation must surely puzzle many readers who examine it in the
light of their own direct knowledge of the poet's work. How, they may
well wonder, can a poet who composed a mass of now unreadable
verses and a handful of exquisite but superficial lyrics on young girls,
roses, and the pleasures of the fleeting moment be counted among the
great poets of France? It is a question seldom expressed, but one likely
to be in the minds of many readers. And rightly so. Knowledge of
Ronsard's work, for those who read French poetry, still depends largely

on some anthology read in school or elsewhere; and in most cases these anthologies, even the most recent, all go back in taste and selection to the time of Sainte-Beuve (about 1830). For most readers, the Ronsard they may know is essentially the poet of the anthologies.

Even if one allows for the importance of the anthologies in the formation of opinions and for the usual time which elapses between scholarly opinion and its general acceptance, how is one to explain the considerable differences between the passionately expressed convictions of a number of scholars concerning the poetry of Ronsard and the fact that these convictions have made so little impression outside a narrow circle of specialists?

First, I suppose, one must acknowledge that the extent of Ronsard's work must discourage all but the most adventuresome and boldest readers. Bewildered at the vastness of the collection before him and unable to know where to begin, the reader flees to the comforting formulas of the guidebook, the manual of literature, the anthology. These certainly can be, and often are, quite useful. But the reader has abandoned his own freedom of selection to the editor. Understandably dismayed at the prospect of finding his way through almost twenty volumes of verse, he turns with relief to some small selection. And so we have the Ronsard of the anthologies.

Should the reader make the unlikely decision to find his own way through the text of Ronsard, he is faced with further perplexities. Which text should be choose? This is not an easy question to answer, for it touches on one of the thorniest problems in modern textual scholarship. Ronsard, during the thirty or more years of his very active life, constantly revised individual poems, sometimes completely transforming them in the course of a series of revisions. Each of the major editions of his complete works published during his lifetime or shortly afterwards shows hundreds of changes in text, in the order of the poems, and in the omission of earlier works. The only edition which enables the reader to follow this complicated artistic process is the critical text begun by Laumonier and continued by Professors Lebègue and Silver.[1] The reprintings of several of Ronsard's collected editions are also available in large libraries, though the only edition of the complete works readily obtainable commercially is that of 1584.[2]

Assuming that he has access to these editions, which text should the reader prefe. The original text published by Ronsard in the first ardor of composition? Some intermediate revision, technically and artistically more refined, but lacking the fire and imagination of the first? The text of 1578, published at the height of his career? The edition of 1584, carefully revised by Ronsard the year before his death? Or finally the posthumous edition of 1587, produced in accordance with the poet's last wishes by his literary executors? Critics are divided in their opinions, not only on the relative merits of each edition, but on the artistic qualities of each single revision in each collection and even in individual poems. It is obviously a problem for which there is no easy solution, and I can only hope to indicate in the course of this study some of the leading opinions of scholars and to indicate the importance of the difficulties raised by the question. Until recently the problem seems to have been generally ignored by compilers of anthologies, who have followed the text of 1584.

Another problem facing the reader, and connected with that just mentioned, is the problem of language. If it is recognized that histories of literature have perhaps exaggerated the importance of Ronsard's linguistic innovations, there still remains the difficulty of sixteenth-century French vocabulary and syntax. The range of Ronsard's vocabulary is vast, the richness of his language impressive. While this richness contributes greatly to the quality of his poetry, it also presents at times undoubted difficulties. Glossaries and lexicons are helpful, and much of the difficulty has been eased by the editors of the critical edition. But in spite of the assistance given by these, the reader must still expect to encounter problems until he develops a feeling for the language of the time.

Changes in language often reflect changes in society in general and in literary tastes in particular. The history of Ronsard's posthumous reputation illustrates the extent to which such changes have affected attitudes toward his poetry. After an eclipse of more than two centuries his reputation was again partially restored by Sainte-Beuve and the Romantics.[3] Their favorite poems were the light "lyric" poems celebrating nature or love, the sonnets to Marie and Hélène which seemed the most personal, and the light odes. Occasionally passages in the longer poems seemed worth saving, especially those recounting Ronsard's poetic autobiography. The taste of 1830 has been surprisingly tenacious; in general it is still reflected in the smaller anthologies today.

With the vastly larger knowledge of the period in which Ronsard lived, the discovery of documents and details of his life, and a study of the literary and philosophical background of his times, scholars gradually opened whole portions of Ronsard's work hitherto neglected: the Pindaric odes, the hymns, the discourses and elegies, and a great number of miscellaneous poems took on new meaning. A whole generation of scholars devoted their knowledge of the ancient humanities and their zeal for Ronsard's poetry to elucidating texts and placing them in the context of Ronsard's life and time. Like every generation they had their own particular strengths and limitations. Our debt to them is so considerable that it would be immodest to cancel it because of things which may seem dated or old-fashioned in the light of more recent literary fashions. Disagreement with their opinions or taste should not imply ingratitude for their labors or disrespect for their scholarship, for it is by such questioning that new facets of Ronsard's work are revealed.[4]

One example, among many, of this change in attitudes toward Ronsard's poetry is a contrast in opinions concerning his use of myth and legend. The criticism of several generations of scholars shows a marked distaste for any but the most obvious references to mythology or ancient legends. Despite, or perhaps because of, their own extensive classical education, these critics often failed to distinguish between second-hand erudition (of which Ronsard is not entirely innocent) and the integration of feeling and thought of the Graeco-Roman world into the realm of the poet's own universe so often achieved by means of a language and symbolism widely accepted by his contemporaries. As a study of the academies of sixteenth-century France has shown, myth and fable were not a dead ornament, but a living language: . . . "the Renaissance had at its disposal a repertory of images, systematized by learned experts, which formed a language used by art and literature in all European countries in which the learning of the humanists had penetrated. The way in which these images were understood linked them vitally to the symbols of religion. Life flowed into them; from above through the contact with the dynamics of a living religion; from all sides, through the enriching commerce between poets, artists, architects, musicians, moving about their appointed tasks within a homogenous culture."[5] Not only was Ronsard using this "universal language," he was expressing a very personal awareness of the meaning of ancient myths and divinities. More than most poets of the time he was independent of the handbooks of mythology. His vast learning was largely gathered at the ancient sources themselves. Commenting on the unique relation between Ronsard and the gods of Olympus, a recent student of the survival of this ancient tradition points to the vitality and conviction which animate Ronsard's myths. In the great numbers of bookish references one senses the pulse of life, and "learning comes to life and is transfigured. In the true sense of the word, the poet lives in a state of *enthusiasm*: he is haunted by these divinities, who from his earliest youth have accompanied his footsteps 'au profond des vallées' and under the 'ombrage incertain' of the forest. The confused, ill-digested mythology with which he has gorged himself does not stifle his imagination, but rather exalts it, for within that mythology there vibrates for him the deep pulse of nature."[6] One can only welcome such an understanding of the importance and uniqueness of myth in the poetry of Ronsard.

The use of myth and legend is one aspect of an even broader question: What is the importance of literary sources and influences in the poetry of Ronsard? For some time it has been a fashion in literary criticism to dismiss as irrelevant interest in the biography, intellectual milieu, and literary antecedents of writers. This is particularly true with regard to a study of the authors of a past age who may have influenced the writer or whom he consciously chose as guides. At one time, perhaps, excessive attention was paid to the "sources" of individual lines or passages in the work of Renaisance poets. Certainly that day is past. Many critics no longer possess the classical education which would enable them to indulge in such erudition. The "sourciers" have done their work. But the larger problem which their patient labor raises must still be answered. With his program for the renewal of French poetry through a carefully limited creative imitation of ancient authors, Ronsard places the matter of "sources" in the fore. His selection of favorite authors, from ancient and modern times, can tell us a great deal about his own taste, his feelings, and his temperament. It may be possible to ignore the antecedents of a Dadaist poem made by drawing words at random from a hat. For a poet with Ronsard's esthetic ideal, it is impossible. Certainly one can read and appreciate the light lyric poems without a thought of Anacreon, Theocritus, or Horace. But without some knowledge of the literary heritage which Ronsard claimed as his own, it is impossible to appreciate the scope of his undertaking, to evaluate his successes or failures, and to realize the interplay of tradition and renewal which is one of the keys to a reading of his vast accomplishment.

Other aspects of Ronsard's poetry take on new meaning and perspective when placed within the intellectual movements of his day. The encyclopedic tradition of Florentine humanism, the influence of the work of Ficino, and the French academies of the Valois are important movements of the time in which Ronsard lived. He was intimately concerned with these movements and the men who led them. One can not fully appreciate the odes without realizing that they were all meant to be sung. Many of the sonnets and short lyrics were set to music by Ronsard's contemporaries and played their part in the great concert of the renewal of all the fine arts and the sciences. An increasing awareness of the importance of the plastic arts and the often difficult comparisons between the poetry of the time and the architects, painters, and sculptors of the first school of Fontainebleau open new horizons. All this rich ferment of artistic and intellectual life forms an essential part of the life of Ronsard which vibrates in his verse.[7]

In an introductory study it would be impossible to give adequate attention to all these facets of the life and times of Ronsard. I can only endeavor to indicate some of the most important connections between his poetry and the intellectual and artistic milieu in which he moved, and to suggest reading for those who wish to pursue the subject. Doubtless I shall fail to give due attention to certain aspects which might be considered essential by some, and place undue emphasis on others. My hope is that the reader will, in spite of these shortcomings, realize the rich possibilities which remain to be explored in a work so filled with unexpected beauty, mystery, and delight.

CHAPTER 2

Page, Scholar, and Poet

Bref, quelquepart que j'erre,
Tant le Ciel m'y soit dous,
Ce petit coin de terre
Me rira par-sus tous.

Les Louanges de Vandomois

I   *Countryside and Court*

PIERRE DE RONSARD was born at the family manor house La Possonnière in the Vendômois, probably in September 1524. Through his mother he was related to a number of ancient families in the region of Touraine and Anjou. His father's family had been wardens of the forest of Gastine and landowners in the province for generations. Recently their position had risen through favor at court. Through his father's successes in the Italian wars and the alliance with the Chaudrier family the young Ronsard seemed to have an established place in the ranks of the provincial gentry and a future position at court.

While Pierre was still an infant his father, Louis de Ronsart, spent four years in Madrid as governer of the household of the sons of François I; the young princes, hostages in place of their father, were held for ransom until the treaty which released them was signed in 1528. Louis de Ronsart is known to have idled away the long hours of this stay by composing poems in the style of the time, the ballades and rondeaux of the *rhetoriqueurs*. The cultural interests of this soldier-poet in the renewal of the arts are still visible today at his estate, where the visitor may see over the windows and doors the Latin mottoes carved into the stone when the chateau was rebuilt in the curiously attractive style of the early Renaissance. The mottoes themselves are representative of that mingling of the medieval, Christian heritage and the new spirit of pagan humanism characteristic of the period: "Domine conserva me" (Preserve me, O God; Psalm xv); "Respice finem" (Think of thy last day); "Tibi sola gloria" (To Thee be all praise) and "Veritas filia temporis" (Truth the daughter of time); "Voluptati et Graciis" (To Pleasure and the Graces). Over the magnificent fireplace in the great hall, one of the finest of the period, may be seen among the rich decorative carvings the coats-of-arms of the lords of the province, of families related to the Ronsarts, and the family motto: "Non falunt futura merentem" (Future rewards will not be lacking to the deserving).

Here in this manor house and in the surrounding countryside Pierre, the youngest of four children, spent the first eleven years of his life. Though it was customary for authors to identify themselves by their city or province, the appearance of *Pierre de Ronsard, Gentilhomme vandomois* on the title pages of his future works seems singularly appropriate. For this countryside along the banks of the Loire, this land of forest and glade, of caves and vineyards and fields, was to mark Ronsard for life. The provinces of Touraine, Maine, Anjou, and his native Vendômois were in a peculiar way the cradle of the French Renaissance. The fiefs and priories of the family dotted the region, whose subtle charm cast a spell over Ronsard which drew him back throughout his life to its familiar scenes, scenes which he was to celebrate in many of his finest poems.[1]

What is known of Ronsard's early life is rather meager. We know that he was christened at the parish church of Couture, the village nearby; the mutilated tombs of his parents still lie in the sanctuary his father helped to restore. We know that he spent an unprofitable term at the Collège de Navarre in Paris in 1533-34. We know that from his uncle, the vicar of Bessé-sur-Braye, he inherited a rather fine collection of books. Aside from the marriage of a sister, we have little other information. All the rest is conjecture and supposition about what sort of education the younger son of an ambitious country nobleman of the time might receive. It is tempting to surmise that the young Ronsard took a less-than-average interest in his studies, judging from his sudden withdrawal from formal studies at the age of ten. One is further tempted to speculate on his pursuits in the countryside, for his poems are filled with country lore and a knowledge of the ways of nature seen at first hand. But all this must remain in the realm of speculation.

In 1536, at the age of twelve, Ronsard began a new life. Escorted by his father he went to Avignon to join the French court and royal army there and to begin his life as an apprentice courtier. His first master was François, eldest son of François I. Only a few days after becoming page to the dauphin, Ronsard saw his master's sudden death, followed rapidly by an autopsy; and by the trial, torture, and execution (on a charge of the poisoning) of the prince's Italian squire. The specter of death which haunts so many of his verses was already a reality in Ronsard's life.

Ronsard's next master was Charles, Duc d'Orléans, third son of the king. While in his service Ronsard was present at the courtship and marriage festivities of James V of Scotland and Madeleine de France, the sister of his master. Following their wedding on New Year's Day in Notre-Dame-de-Paris, Ronsard entered the household of the French princess and sailed with her to Scotland in May. His stay was brief, for the new queen of Scots died in August. Her household, dressed in mourning, returned to France. In December of the same year Ronsard, attached to a special diplomatic mission, again set out for Scotland, where another French noblewoman, Marguerite de Guise, had become the bride of James V. This time the party traveled by way of Flanders through the rich trading cities of the Spanish Netherlands. Their crossing of the North Sea was a near disaster; within sight of the port the vessel nearly sank in a heavy storm. Once settled at the Scottish court Ronsard may have met a young Italian nobleman mentioned by the earliest biographers as "le seigneur Paul" and generally identified as Claudio Duchi. Whether they met in Holyrood Palace or later is unimportant; the importance of their friendship lies in Duchi's initiating Ronsard into the Latin poets who most profoundly marked his own poetic development: Vergil and Horace. In the spring the French mission returned by way of England, visiting the court of Henry VIII. His stay in Britain seems to have left few traces in the poetry of Ronsard, but the introduction to the finest poets of Rome, either there or in France, awakened in him a curiosity and desire which would eventually become the dominant quest of his life.

Ronsard was now fifteen, too old to remain a page. To prepare for the next step of his career he entered the Écurie Royale, the Royal Riding School located at the Tournelles near the present Place des Voges. This was no mere stable, but an academy and a school for young noblemen, training them in knightly accomplishments and in the knowledge they would need at court or in the royal service. This was the meeting place of artisans and craftsmen, of harnessmakers, silversmiths, and saddlers. At this academy, directed by François de Carnavalet, Ronsard perfected his natural gifts for riding, jumping, and handling weapons under the eye of the most skillful masters in the kingdom.[2] One of his companions-in-arms was the future Henri II. Another was the same Claudio Duchi who spent more time reading Latin poets than in the ring learning to ride. There can be no doubt that, reared as he was to admire the military life and with his strong and supple build, Ronsard was soon apt and ready to follow the career of courtier and soldier for which his father seems to have prepared him.

Once again attached to the household of Charles d'Orléans, Ronsard was sent in the summer of 1540 to accompany a French mission to Haguenau in Alsace. There the French, led by the scholar and diplomat Lazare de Baïf, held a conference with the representatives of German Protestant princes. The spokesmen for both parties were scholars and humanists who expressed themselves in the elegant phrases of ciceronian Latin. Keeping such company must have been an impressive experience for a young man of Ronsard's curiosity and ambition.

At the end of the summer when the mission returned to Paris, Ronsard's career took another abrupt turn. After a severe fever Ronsard remained half-deaf. The fever, probably malarial, was recurrent and left him weak and exhausted. He withdrew from the court and from the Écurie Royale to his father's estate where he began the slow convalescence leading to partial recovery.

Can we be sure, as most of Ronsard's biographers tell us, that this fever and the hardness of hearing which followed led the nineteen-year-old Ronsard to turn immediately to poetry? Are we being misled by Ronsard's own desire to impress us with his early poetic vocation? Poetry had been the pastime of his father, now nearly seventy. And it was the amusement of a number of Renaissance gentlemen. But it was not a means of livelihood in an age when most of the property went to the eldest son, when inflation was making the lives of the gentry financially difficult, and when poets were at the mercy of patrons.

Ronsard tells us in a poem written in 1560 (and the examples of many of his contemporaries bear it out) that these younger sons of provincial noblemen were encouraged to pursue legal studies, whether in civil or canon law, in order to find a lucrative post in the royal or ecclesiastical courts of law. It is notable that it was only after his father's death in 1544 that Ronsard devoted himself to the formal study of Greek and Latin poetry.[3]

Meanwhile Ronsard convalesced and delighted in the rural pleasure so often described in his verse. And he composed his first poems, beginning in Latin but soon turning to French. He and his father must have come to a compromise concerning his future. Together they attended the funeral of a distant cousin, Guillaume de Langey, a distinguished member of the du Bellay family. This famous captain had been a patron of Rabelais, who also attended the funeral ceremonies in the cathedral of Le Mans. Afterwards Ronsard received the simple tonsure of a cleric in minor orders from Langey's brother René du Bellay, diocesan bishop of the Ronsard family. By this act Ronsard became eligible to receive ecclesiastical revenues and income from church endowments and lands. Though never ordained a priest, he remained a celibate churchman for the rest of his life. The gift of many of these benefices was not in the hands of the clergy directly, but, since the Concordat of 1515, in the hands of the crown. Thus Ronsard's future would be subject largely to the whims of courtiers who were able to influence the granting of church livings. The disciple of the Muses, whether he liked it or not, was to be the servant of princes and prelates.

The secretary of the bishop was Jacques Peletier du Mans, who had been present at these ceremonies. He is known to have seen Ronsard's earliest poems and to have encouraged his efforts. He himself had been in touch with a circle of humanists and young poets at the University of Poitiers. Not only did he encourage Ronsard to continue his writing of poetry, but he advised him to become thoroughly familiar with ancient poetry while continuing to write his verse in French. At the time Peletier was engaged in a translation and commentary of Horace's *Epistle to the Pisos* (the Art of Poetry) which he published in 1545. His encouragement and advice must have done much to influence Ronsard's decision to devote himself to poetry; indeed his advice and example set the course that Ronsard would follow for much of his career.

In June 1544 Louis de Ronsart died. The way was open for his son to return to Paris and to undertake the long and toilsome initiation into Greek and Latin letters that he felt essential to prepare himself for the vocation of poet.

II *Ronsard at the* Collège de Coqueret/ *Jean Dorat*

> Sur ma langue doucement
> Tu mis au commencement,
> Je ne sçais quelles merveilles,
> Que vulgaires je rendis
> Et premier les espandis
> Dans les Françoyeses oreilles.
>
> *A son maistre Jan Dorat*

At the age of twenty Ronsard returned to Paris. He seems for some time to have retained his attachment to the court and some sort of pension, for the inheritance from his father's estate was unsettled, and in any case would never have sufficed to support him. His functions allowed ample time for his principal concern, a study and mastery of Greek and Latin Poetry.

The master who directed these studies was, by good fortune, established in the town house of Lazare de Baïf, whom Ronsard had accompanied to Alsace four years previously. Already known as the foremost Hellenist in France, Jean Dorat had been the pupil of Guillaume Budé. His reputation as a scholar and interpreter of Greek texts had secured him the post of tutor to Baïf's young son, Jean-Antoine; eventually he was appointed to the chair of Greek in the Royal College of Readers (the present-day Collège de France). Members of the court and of the French judiciary flocked to his public lectures and to the "academy" which was held in Baïf's house and later at the Collège de Coqueret. A whole generation of pupils have left testimonies in letters and poems to his gifts as a scholar, teacher, and friend. Under his guidance Ronsard achieved a mastery of Greek and Latin poetry equalled by few French poets in any age.[4]

Until 1547 Ronsard shared the private lessons of Dorat with Jean-Antoine de Baïf. Though still a young schoolboy, Baïf was far advanced in his Greek studies, and Ronsard was hard put to keep the pace. About this time Dorat was appointed principal of the small

Collège de Coqueret. When Làzare de Baïf died in the same year, the two young scholars took up residence in the college.

Among the small number of boarding students in the college was a distant relative of Ronsard's, Joachim du Bellay. Like Ronsard he came from the provincial nobility and had been destined for a career at law. Like Ronsard he had met Jacques Peletier, and together with his friends at the University of Poitiers he devoted his time more to poetry than to lawbooks. Shortly after Dorat had become principal of Coqueret, he and Ronsard may have met at an inn where they discovered their common interest. At Ronsard's urging, du Bullay decided to join the pupils of Dorat and prepare himself to compose the "new poetry" envisioned by Peletier.

The Collège de Coqueret was one of nearly one hundred colleges which in the sixteenth century composed the University of Paris. Of these, eighteen were considered "great Colleges," the others "small." At the zenith of its glory in the Middle Ages the University was controlled largely by the faculties. By the end of the fifteenth century these had lost much of their ancient prestige and power; the vacuum was filled by the colleges, which had acquired a kind of autonomy. Thus it was that, for a brief period, the curriculum of an obscure college like Coqueret, directed by a man of Dorat's abilities, could be centered almost exclusively about the humanities, particularly Greek and Latin poetry. A similar curriculum was instituted at the much wealthier and famous Collège de Boncourt, which, thanks to two generations of the Galland family, remained a bastion of the new humanistic studies despite the threats of the Faculty of Theology at the Sorbonne. From these two colleges came most of the poets who formed the "brigade" of young poets who gathered about Ronsard.[5]

Glimpses of life in Coqueret and Boncourt may be found in the early poems of Ronsard and his classmates. The students rose at five or six in the morning, dressed hastily, and began their studies. Later, about eight o'clock, came breakfast. They returned to their books or recitations until dinner at eleven. Following a short time for recreation they recited or read until a light supper at five or six in the evening. A review of the day's work might follow, or an outing in the streets of Paris. They might, if they liked, retire early; if they were eager to make the most of their time, they might like Ronsard spend the late hours bent over their books. A poem of Baïf recalls these labors and gives an idea of the kind of authors studied at Coqueret. If you are looking for Ronsard, he says,

> You will find him bent over Nicander,
> Or Callimachus, or over the ashes
> Of Anacreon, who yet remains
> More precious than gold,
> All hunched over, molding the grace
> Of his features after the ancient
> Pattern of the most secret
> Greek and Roman poets.

Then, Baïf continues, when Ronsard finally went to bed in the early hours of morning, Baïf rose and replaced him at the work table.[6]

The mention of Callimachus, Anacreon, and Nicander gives some notion of the authors studied under Dorat. By the end of his formal education at Coqueret, and for some years afterwards, Ronsard read widely in Greek literature. Either in the original text or in Latin translations he was familiar with all the major, and many of the minor, authors of Greece from the poems of Pindar and Homer to the works of the Hellenistic period. Authors today considered obscure or unimportant were pored over with zealous care: Lycophron, Nicander, Aratus. This Hellenic learning is of first importance in the formation of Ronsard's poetic theory and practice.

The study of Greek texts under Dorat must have been a rare treat, and his teaching an inspiration to his pupils. We know from the most competent scholars of his time that Dorat possessed a rare insight into the textual interpretation of difficult authors such as Pindar and Aeschylus. We know also from the poems of Ronsard that he was the kind of teacher who could kindle in his audience his own enthusiasm for his authors. Before Ronsard left Coqueret the doors of the small college were opened to a larger public: statesmen, prelates, courtiers, and judges crowded the lectures and the "academy" held there.

For his pupils at Coqueret and for the wider public Dorat was not simply a pedagogue of unusual abilities. His knowledge of the humanities extended to the "moral and natural" philosophy which linked the study of poetry with the wider interest of his time: astronomy, mathematics, music, and the arts. The academy, comprising an informal gathering of intellectuals, was the forerunner of those founded later by Baïf and demonstrates the importance of the synthesis of learning, the "encyclopaedia," which was the ideal of the leading minds of the century. These ideals are found in the dialogues of Pontus de Tyard; in those of Guy de Bruès, Ronsard and Baïf appear as speakers. Ronsard's own poetry shows his deep commitment to the speculative "science" which so intrigued his contemporaries. He was never completely out of touch with the leading minds of Paris whom he had first encountered at the "academy" of Dorat.

Dorat was, for his pupils, not only a supreme teacher but a mentor, guide, and companion. Humanist that he was, he insisted on the reading of texts not only for their literary interpretation but also for their moral lessons, which he conveyed by allegorical readings. This tradition goes back through the Middle Ages to antiquity. The episode of Ulysses and Circe, the enchantress in the *Odyssey*, he read as an allegory of the snares of sensual pleasures at first succumbed to and finally overcome. For Dorat poetry might contain a moral truth hidden from the eyes of the uninitiated beneath the veil of ornament and fable. Similar concepts are echoed in the prefaces of Ronsard and in his poetry.

Life at Coqueret was not all study and no games. Like Rabelais' hero Gargantua, the students and principal of the college enjoyed excursions into the country around Paris. During the sixteenth century there was a complete contrast between the noisy, smelly city, still crowded within its medieval walls, and the rustic countryside outside the gates. On occasions the entire college prepared for a whole day's outing. One of these is described in detail in one of Ronsard's most delightful poems: *Le Folastrissime voyage d'Harcueil* (The Frolicsome Excursion to Arcueil). The poem is animated by movement and *brio,* tales of pranks and bravado, Gallic feasting and collegiate erudition. It is a remarkably artistic rendering of the full-blooded Renaissance of Ronsard's youth. The students and staff of the college, led by their principal, leave at dawn, loaded with wine and other provisions for their picnic. Ronsard greets the day with an elaborate classical salutation and then proceeds to portray the rowdy and exuberant students as they make their way to the Seine near Paris. The verse form with its rapid movement and echoing rhyme is ideal for rendering both the high spirits of the feast and the classical erudition which accompanies it. Here are several passages describing the feast:

Let each one seize a branch
    In his hand!
Let each one in a lively voice
Deafen the countryside,
    The mountains,
The streams, fields, and woods!
Now the lighted kitchen fire
    Sends its smoke
Leaping to the heavens,
Now the tables all set up
    Groan beneath
A delicious festive load.

. . . .

Be prodigal, spread around
    The meat
With a generous hand,
And the wines with which the queen
    Of Memphis
Feasted the indolent Roman.

. . . .

Lo! let's drink, let's sing,
    Let's charm
The tooth of fretful cares!
For thieving old age
    Already treads
Upon the back of our heels.[7]

These years under Dorat, and the continuing relations with enthusiastic students and humanist professors at neighboring colleges, the associations with the intellectual and social elite of Paris left an indelible mark on Ronsard. His great love of the world of ancient poetry and of the living qualities of natural forces and of the gods that move them, his devotion to learning, his zest for the enjoyment of the pleasures of good cheer and lively company: all these he carried with him into his poetry. They go far toward explaining why his first volume of poems is considered a turning point in the history of French letters, and why his contemporaries bestowed on him a title he still bears, the prince of poets.

CHAPTER 3

War Against the Monster Ignorance

Celuy qui ne nous honore
Comme Prophetes des Dieux
Plein d'un orgueil odieux
Les Dieux il mesprise encore
Et le Ciel qui nous decore
De son tresor le plus beau,
Nous mariant au troupeau
Que le saint Parnasse adore.

A Joachim du Bellay, Angevin

1 *Ronsard's Conception of Poetry*

NOT long after the accession of Henri II to the French throne two books appeared which mark a turning point in the history of French letters: du Bellay's *Deffence et Illustration de la Langues Françoyse*, together with the first version of his sonnet sequence *L'Olive* and his *Vers lyriques* (1549); and Ronsard's *Quatre Premiers Livres des Odes*, together with earlier poems under the title *Le Bocage* (1550). These two books mark the open claim of the poets of the new generation for the renewal of French poetry by rejecting the past and turning elsewhere than Gaul for their inspiration. Arts of poetry and collections of verse with manifestoes as prefaces were not new to France. But these books were different. They claimed to inaugurate something quite foreign and rained undisguised scorn on the rhymesters of the older tradition, writers of *virelais*, rondeaux, ballades, "and other rubbish of that sort." They made a clarion call for a return to the ideals of ancient poetry.

The exact role of Ronsard in the inception and composition of the *Deffence* is uncertain, though without a doubt he was one of du

Bellay's closest collaborators. The manifesto bears unmistakable signs of hasty, and often confused, organization. Certain ideas remain ambiguous; others are disconnected by long digressions. Whole passages are almost translated verbatim from an Italian treatise on a similar subject. But in the main it seems certain that the concept of poetry, and the program to be followed in its renewal, were shared by both du Bellay and Ronsard. At the time it appeared, they had been bound by common ties for at least two years; they shared the same master at Coqueret, a common heritage, and above all an enthusiasm for a new ideal, and a youthful confidence in their own abilities to fulfill it. This enthusiasm and reckless confidence go far to save the *Deffence* from the defects mentioned above and contribute to the tone of militant urgency which still sounds in its pages.

In addition to the *Deffence*, which may be assumed to express Ronsard's opinions on important matters concerning poetry, his ideal of the poet and his poetry may be found in prefaces and in numerous passages of his poetry, beginning with the first odes and continuing into the posthumous preface and poems published in 1587. These expressions in prose and verse cover the entire range of his career and vary in tone and content, from idealized accounts of his own poetic formation to acerbic attacks on his opponents at court and on enemies in religious and political controversies. His one prose work on poetry, *Abrégé de l'Art Poètique françois*, was hastily written in 1565 at the request of a young admirer, the son of a naturalized Italian poet. Many of Ronsard's most penetrating statements on his concept of poetry are to be found scattered through his poetry.

The *Abrégé* opens with lofty generalities and concludes with fairly detailed notes on French versification. The opening is much more consonant with the statements found in poems and may serve as an introduction to Ronsard's concepts. These concepts, like those of his contemporaries at Coqueret and Boncourt, show the strong influence of Neoplatonic thought so marked in the intellectual circles of the mid-sixteenth century. For its influence on poetry, the dialogue of Plato's most important for these concepts of poetry is the *Ion*, which had been available in the Greek text for some time, as well as in Latin and Italian versions. In 1546 it was translated into French by Richard le Blanc, whose preface is a close rendering of the commentary by Marsilio Ficino. This fifteenth-century humanist had attempted in his elaborate commentaries on the works of Plato to achieve a synthesis of Platonic thought with medieval science and philosophy and Christian doctrine. However strange this synthesis may appear to the modern mind, it exercised a great attraction on the thought of Ronsard's contemporaries. Aspects of it appear in the poetry of Maurice Scève, Heroët, and Pontus de Tyard, all of whom were known to Ronsard. It appears in the poems of du Bellay and is one of the concepts which underlies the founding of Baïf s academy later in the century.

For Ronsard, poetry was a divine gift which the Muses (agents of divinity) bestowed mysteriously upon those whom they had chosen to be the recipients of this scared trust. Without this gift no amount of study or art could make of an ordinary mortal a true poet. Inspired by this divine fury, the poet might become a prophet, a seer, an interpreter of the mysteries of the gods and of the universe. Though the poet received this gift through no merit of his own, just as the Christian receives grace, he should endeavor to be worthy of the gift and to make use of it in the proper way. Here is a portrait of the true poet drawn by du Bellay in the *Deffence*: After receiving divine inspiration, he had prepared himself by study and a virtuous life to fulfill his task, ". . . endowed with an excellent felicity of nature, learned in all good Arts and Sciences, principally the natural and mathematical, versed in all styles of the best Greek and Latin authors, not ignorant of the duties and functions of human life, not of too high birth, nor yet too humble and poor, not disturbed by domestic matters, but of a calm and restful mind, a tranquility acquired through the greatness of his heart, then maintained by his own prudent and wise control. . . " (*Deffence* ed. Chamard, pp. 127-28; Livre II, ch. v). Ronsard seems to recall this ideal of the poet in his *Abrégé* of 1565. He begins by showing the supremacy of the gifts of nature in forming the true poet, then warns the aspiring poet of his moral responsibilities: "Above all things you will hold the Muses in reverence, indeed in special veneration, and will never cause them to serve low and ridiculous causes, nor insulting libels, but you will always cherish them as sacred, as the daughters of Jupiter, that is of God, who, through his holy grace, first revealed through them to ignorant peoples the excellences of his favor." After a history of poetry from earliest times, from divine poets to the human but inspired Greeks, the "laborious" Romans, Ronsard continues: "And so, since the Muses are unwilling to dwell in a soul, unless it be good, holy, and virtuous, you will be of a kindly nature, not wicked, churlish, or ill-tempered; but, moved by a noble spirit, you will allow nothing to enter your mind that is not above the basely human . . . " (*Abrégé de l'Art Poëtique françois;* Laum. XIV, 4-5).

However exaggerated this may appear to the modern reader, it is nevertheless an ideal which reflects Ronsard's lofty concept of the poetic mission and makes a strong contrast with the merely workman-like notion of poetry as a craft, a simple branch of rhetoric, which had for so long dominated in France.

The contrast between nature and art, so pronounced in certain Renaissance treatises on poetry, is found in Ronsard as well, particular-ly in the earlier poems. In certain expressions of it the contrast seems almost absolute. In later passages the two are seen as different aspects of creation, though Ronsard never uses this word. In no case does Ronsard ever see the gifts of nature as secondary to art, but one can trace in Ronsard's opinions, and in his own practice, a gradual recognition of the importance of skill and craftsmanship in the creation of poetry.

The *Deffence* makes the importance of study and laborious application quite clear. "It is useless," says du Bellay, "to claim that because poets are born, further effort and learning are unrequired. Certainly it would be too easy, and therefore worthless, to win eternal fame if a natural felicity were sufficient for performing a task worthy of immortality. Whoever wishes [his works] to pass through the hands and the mouths of men must remain closed within his room for long hours: and whoever wishes to live in the memory of posterity must, as though dead to self, sweat and tremble many a time; and just as court poets drink, eat and sleep as they please, he must endure hunger, thirst and long night vigils" (*Deffence*, ed. Chamard, pp 105-6; Livre II, ch. iii). The insistence on hard work and learning and the contrast between the true poet and the idle, ignorant drone at court could not be clearer.

What is the nature of this poetry for which the poet has been prepared by divine inspiration and long study, and how does the poet go about writing it? In his answer to these questions Ronsard does not use our modern expression "literary creation," for in his time creation was considered an act proper only to God. Rather he uses several words to describe various aspects of the creative act, each word, in a way, being part of the function of the other. (An analogous way of describing a function or problem may be seen in the *Essays* of Montaigne.) In the section of the *Abrégé* entitled "De l'Invention" he says: "Invention is nothing other than the right use of natural endowment of imagination which conceives the Ideas and forms of all things that can be imagined, both celestial and terrestrial, animate and inanimate, so as to represent, describe, and imitate them: for just as the goal of the orator is to persuade, so that of the Poet is to imitate, invent, and represent things which are, which can be, or which can be true-seeming. And there is no doubt, that after right and noble invention of a thing, the fine order of verses will follow, inasmuch as disposition follows invention, the mother of all things, just as the shadow follows the body" (*Abrégé,* Laum. XIV, 13; text of 1567-73).

It is clear from this passage, and from similar statements in his poetry, that Ronsard, while never separating subject from form, placed primary emphasis on the significant content of poetry; and that for him the formal arrangement, choice of words and epithets, images, rhymes, and rhythm were the consequent, and subordinate, elements in literary creation. The poetic instinct, the mysterious aspect never defined by Ronsard, will lead the true poet to this first and most crucial choice; the succeeding ones, about which Ronsard and du Bellay give much detailed advice, may be learned by the careful observation of the natural world and by the example of the best poets.

Like many Renaissance poets Ronsard thought of himself as a portrayer and imitator of nature. Like his contemporaries he takes the term "nature" in the widest possible sense. Following the Aristotelian concept, he says that the task of the poet is to imitate nature in all its diversity. This is not mere reproducing of particular objects, but the rendering of what seems true of them and the relating of this particular aspect to universal truth. Whereas many poets and theorists of the time, following Horace, failed to see the broad import of Aristotle's view of imitation and thought of it in terms of mere vivid representation, Ronsard seems to have sensed and preserved some of Aristotle's original intention.[1]

The real significance of nature for Ronsard, it seems to me, is his feeling for its enormous richness and diversity. In the "Au Lecteur" of the *Odes* of 1550 he says: "I am of the opinion that no Poetry should be held praiseworthy or finished unless it represents nature, which was esteemed beautiful by the ancients only because it is inconstant and variable in its perfections" (Laum. I, 47). This admiration of variety and richness in nature is a key to the understanding of Ronsard's own poetry; he never ceases to profess that abundance and variety are his ideals. It is, in fact, the pursuit of these ideals, and the achievement of them, that gives Ronsard's own poems the dazzling and often disconcerting variety of styles, manner, and forms which he rightly considered the mark of a great poet.

If the representation of what is true or potentially true in nature is the poet's goal, how is he to be guided in attaining it? The poet's inspiration, his study, his cultivation of ethical and moral values prepare him for his task, but he must still render his vision in an acceptable and artistic manner. It is at this juncture that Ronsard arrived at a paradoxical solution new to French literature: the best guides for the representation of nature were the ancient Greek and Roman poets and their Italian imitators. Thus creative imitation of these authors is the cardinal principle of the new poetry. Ronsard's insistence on the excellence of the ancients, and particularly the Greeks, as guides and models, was the most revolutionary and controversial aspect of the theory and practice of the new poets.[2] Coupled with Ronsard's insistence on writing in the native language, the theory of the assimilation and re-creation of the Graeco-Latin poetic heritage was the hallmark of the new school. Though the theory of imitation was never free from the temptation to copy in a servile way, it did open to the vernacular literature of France a great wealth of poetic booty which was eagerly accepted by the young poets of Ronsard's "brigade" and gradually assimilated into the national heritage.

The young poets were bold, and in fact presumptuous, to challenge the traditions of generations.[3] Their challenge did not go unheeded. Having thrown down the gauntlet, they prepared to show that they could produce the new poetry as well as describe it. Ronsard's first entry into the battle against "the hideous monster of Ignorance" was his four books of *Odes*.

II *The Publication of the* Odes *(1550)*

Moisi du temps ton bois ne sonnoit point;
Lors j'eu pitié de te voir mal-en-point,
Toy qui jadis des grands Rois les viandes
Fasois trouver plus douces et friandes.
Pour te monter de cordes et d'un fust,

Voire d'un son qui naturel te fust,
Je pillay Thebe et saccageay la Pouille,
T'enrichissant de leur belle despouille.

Ode à sa Lyre[4]

The publication of Ronsard's four books of *Odes* marks his debut as
the self-proclaimed leader of a new group of poets in France. Already
heralded with lavish praise in du Bellay's *Deffence* and in his *Vers
lyriques* published the previous year, Ronsard's volume was anticipated
by friendly and hostile members of the world of letter. The odes,
"measured to the lyre," and the miscellaneous earlier lyric poems which
he no longer deemed worthy of that title and relegated to the *Bocage,*
are accompanied by laudatory verse in Greek, Latin, and French
composed for the occasion by admirers, who included Dorat and du
Bellay.

The same air of militant confidence which animates the pages of the
Deffence reaches its peak in Ronsard's preface. The pretentions of the
new poets, their parade of learning, their scorn of the medieval French
tradition and the followers of Marot had already been answered by
several writers. Ronsard makes no attempt to conciliate the hostile, or
even moderate, public, nor to paliate his strictures against ignorance.
Rather he makes it clear that he writes only for the learned, and true
lovers of poetry. Finding the French tradition sterile, he turned
elsewhere for inspiration. "I sought [it] among strangers, and became a
companion of Horace, imitating his natural sweetness, at the same time
that Clément Marot (in those years the only light of vernacular poetry)
was laboring at the completion of his Psalter [1542] . . . " (Laum. I,
44). From this time, he continues, with the encouragement of his
friends he had endeavored to endow France with a new form, the ode,
which he claims to introduce both in name and in fact. Further he
claims to have shunned the imitation of French authors, ". . . treading a
path hitherto unknown, and showing the way to follow Pindar and
Horace," his two principal models. Taking his inspiration from the
ancient Greek concept of the union of music and poetry, Ronsard
further claims to have revived this ancient art and to have introduced it
to the French. With the exception of the earliest odes, which he has
placed in the section called *Bocage*, all the poems in the new collection
are "measured to the lyre"; that is, each stanza, or group of stanzas,

follows the same metrical pattern, so that each corresponding stanza may be sung to the same musical setting. This is no purely academic claim, for in the second edition the music for the settings, composed by leading musicians of the time, is printed after the text. This painstaking composition of strophic forms with the express intention of musical performance was fundamental to Ronsard's concept of lyric poetry at the opening of his career. While it is undoubtedly true that he neither introduced the word nor the concept of "ode" into France as he claimed, he deserves at least the credit of realizing the full implication of the humanist ideal of music as the affective art binding all the sciences and arts together. In concluding his truculent preface, Ronsard claims the right as a poet to praise not only others, but himself, just as Pindar had done. For it is the poet, he says, the prophet and interpreter of the Muses, whose verses bestow immortality. As for the envious and unlearned, they are dismissed as unworthy of his attention. So ends this preface. The war on the "Monster Ignorance," already threatened in du Bellay's manifesto and the poems of 1549, has been fully declared.

III *Pindaric Odes*

> Je te veil bastir une ode
> La maçonnant à la mode
> De tes palais honnorés,
> Qui volontiers ont l'entrée
> De grands marbres acoustrée
> Et de haus piliers dorés'[5]

The poems which compose the odes of 1550, and subsequent revisions and amplifications, are arranged in a poetic, not a chronological, order. The earliest poems, at first removed to a section called the *Bocage*, were composed before Ronsard insisted on the strict metrical form which permitted complete musical settings. These, composed as early as 1542, are largely Horatian in inspiration. Later under the influence of Dorat he began the composition of odes arranged in the manner of Pindar and using certain themes and images borrowed from the great Theban poet. These Pindaric odes form the façade of Ronsard's collection. Like the elaborate doorways of the Renaissance they are meant to form an imposing entrance to the entire work. For the Pindaric ode is one of Ronsard's boldest and most ambitious attempts to illustrate the "new" poetry. After the Pindaric odes come all the others, each book being arranged in the same order of precedence: first the poems dedicated to the king and to members of the royal family; next those dedicated to the great nobility and powerful persons at court; then less formal poems sent to friends and fellow poets; and finally a group of odes on various themes long associated with lyric verse, such as love, drinking songs, praise of homeland, and so on.

In his preface Ronsard had boasted of tuning the Theban and Apulian lyre to French words; he had, in fact, placed his collection under the dual patronage of the master of the Greek ode, Pindar, and the most skillful and elegant composer of Latin odes, Horace. From his own statements, and an observation of his entire work, it is clear that Horace remained Ronsard's most congenial and most deeply appreciated guide. His studies at Coqueret had introduced him as well to the magnificent poetry of Pindar, who for a while became his great inspiration. So it is with these Pindaric poems that he opens his collection.

In addition to the two principal guides of the odes Ronsard drew from his vast reading in many other sources of inspiration. One could almost draw up a list of the authors read in the most learned circles of Paris by glancing through the notes of a critical edition of the odes: ancient Greek lyric poets, the tragedians, the Alexandrians; Latin poets, chiefly Vergil and Horace, but also a score of others; Italians writing both in Latin and their vernacular, including Petrarch and his imitators. The scope of Ronsard's reading is impressive; the temptation to borrow and to translate must have been considerable. And indeed one can find examples of this unfortunate corollary of the theory of imitation. In a number of instances phrases and whole passages are free translations. But if this were all, Ronsard would not be a great poet and the *Odes* would not inaugurate a new poetry.[6]

One might make a whole book of examples of Ronsard's use of older poetry for the creation of something new, fresh, and quite French in tone. While several of the odes of 1550 are simply free version of odes by Pindar or Horace (more frequently the latter) the usual process is more complicated: Ronsard combines skillfully the theme of one passage with similar themes or images from another passage, perhaps in the same poem, or from another poem by the same author, perhaps from an entirely different poet, adding as he goes the connecting links, the changes in style and expression, in image and metaphor, which transform the borrowed fragments sometimes beyond recognition. This process of combining and transforming passages freely adapted in French with passages of his own work (called "contamination des textes") is perhaps the most commonly misunderstood practice of Ronsard's time, one which is the very basis of his art. Unless one accepts the notion that the poet is not bound to be "original" in theme, but rather to restate common themes in a new way, he will never appreciate Renaissance poetry, or art. Beginning with the odes and ending with the *Derniers Vers*, Ronsard's entire *oeuvre* is an illustration of this principle.

As one might expect, this technique is more obvious in an early collection like the odes of 1550. Then Ronsard was still eager to parade his considerable learning in classical literature. Later, like Montaigne, he says little about his models, hoping to catch his critics who, in attacking him, are in reality condemning as well an ancient poet whom they have failed to recognize. To study the odes is to realize the importance of this technique in the "illustration de la langue française." Paradoxically it was this apparently unoriginal method of introducing foreign texts from the great poets of the Graeco-Latin tradition which enabled Ronsard and his contemporaries to achieve a new loftiness and elegance in French poetry which has rarely been equalled.

It has been customary to divide the odes of 1550 into two main groups, Pindaric and Horatian. This division is certainly suggested by Ronsard's own arrangement, and it offers a convenient way of approaching the collection. Those odes whose stanzas are grouped in one or more triads (strophe, antistrophe, and epode) are called Pindaric: others are called Horatian or Anacreontic. Actually this division can be misleading. The influence of Horace is quite apparent in the Pindaric odes. This is only natural in view of Horace's own intention of adapting the Greek lyric ode to his own language. The Latin poet was consciously creating from Greek models, and one of his models, though not a chief one, was Pindar. Though in many ways the opposite of Pindar, in personality, attitude, and style, Horace approaches on occasion the grandeur and sobriety of the Greek poet. Conversely in the later Horatian odes the influence of Pindar can still be felt, particularly in passages in which Ronsard alludes to his role as a poet-seer and to his inspiration. It is this complexity of inspiration and its interplay with Ronsard's own creative genius which adds richness, variety, and breadth to the collection.

From the moment of their publication until today critics have never tired of repeating the faults of the Pindaric odes. Ronsard is accused of obscurity, pedantry, bombast, insincerity, artificiality, and worst of all, tiresomeness. Sainte-Beuve in his somewhat timid rehabilitation of the poets of the sixteenth century found these odes "unreadable." More recent critics have more often than not confirmed the opinions of their predecessors, though with perhaps more nuance and discrimination in their judgments.

Why, critics wonder, did Ronsard come to choose Pindar as a model of his new poetic form? The influence of Dorat, his master and guide in Greek and Roman letters, is a likely answer; for Dorat is known to have written Pindaric odes in Latin and may have known of similar poems in Italian. (These Italian poets, writing either in Latin or the vernacular, may well have been as influential as Pindar in the formation of the French Pindaric ode.)[7]

For whatever reasons Ronsard may have chosen Pindar, critics have been nearly unanimous in finding this choice a false step, a betrayal of Ronsard's "natural talent" (whatever that may mean) into which he was led by youthful vanity and enthusiasm for a display of erudition. This first mistake led to others and to the failure of Ronsard's efforts. Critics note that the archaic Greek society for which Pindar's odes were written and performed was too dissimilar from the France of the Valois kings. What indeed, they ask, do poems celebrating the victories of athletes in ancient games have to do with the lords and ladies of the court of Henri II and Catherine de Medici? Furthermore, the form of the Greek choral ode, whose divisions marked the movement of the dance which accompanied the musical declamation, was totally inappropriate to French prosody. The allusive and occasionally obscure mythology of Pindar, perhaps clear to his own audience, was beyond the comprehension of even the most erudite Renaissance public. Then too, the critics add, Pindar himself is too much aware of his role as a prophet and spokesman of the gods. If Pindar's descriptions of the "poetic fury" are forced, Ronsard's appear completely false, and his pretensions of conferring immortality on those he praises are offensive. Added to all these strictures is the famous "beau désordre," the elegant disorder supposed by the neoclassical critics to characterize the illogical arrangement and episodic form of the Pindaric ode. Finally the peculiar gnomic phrases and metaphors, so foreign to the "genius of the French language" and tradition, give a bizarre and alien cast to the expression.

As if all these reasons were not sufficient to fault Ronsard's poems from the outset, critics have found other flaws. The text of Pindar, they point out, was even more of an enigma for the Renaissance scholar than for the classicist of today. Following the Byzantine tradition Renaissance editors divided the strophes into long stanzas with many short lines. Ronsard, in slavishly following this arrangement, failed to attain the gravity of tone which would have been possible in a more ample line, such as the Alexandrine.

In spite of all these defects, critics do concede some merit to the Pindaric odes. With all their faults the odes are considered by literary historians as the beginning of the great lyric tradition in French poetry. Occasionally, we are told, thanks to Ronsard's genius, a note of true grandeur sounds through all the mythology and forced rhetoric. At times, they concede, Ronsard achieves a mastery of rhythm and sound unique for his time (but, by implication, far surpassed in later periods). Finally, looking back at the odes through the accomplishments of more modern poets, critics see the odes' true function: to prepare the way for later generations. Typical of these judgments are two statements of Cohen. The first is a comment on the disappointing "grandeur" of the odes: "The Pindaric odes always give us the impression of a bird with a wounded wing which attempts an ambitious flight without being able to remain at a lofty height. . . ." Later, the same critic sees the true value of Ronsard as that of a precursor, a kind of John the Baptist for Victor Hugo: "Ronsard laid out the ethereal path on which Hugo was later to soar without effort."[8]

No one would deny that there is truth in these judgments, but it is not the whole truth. It is true that Ronsard made mistakes in choice of subject and in the composition of the poems. Similarly, certain evaluations of the odes seem justified: one can easily select passages to prove each point. The Pindaric odes are indeed a façade constructed with great artifice, a façade which leads to some of Ronsard's finest poetry. As such they need not detain the person who is impatient to go further into the storehouse of Ronsard's work. But the problems raised by the kind of criticism they have generally received are so basic to much of Ronsard's "serious" verse that they call for attention at the very outset.

The first thing that might be noted is that the critics from the beginning seem to have decided that the odes were unsuccessful and then searched for reasons to explain the failure. Since the odes are Pindaric, the fault must lie in the choice of Pindar as a model, with the differences between his poetry and society and those of Ronsard being the main source of difficulties. These differences were quite real, as were similar differences in the case of other poets imitated by Ronsard. But there were similarities as well. Pindar's lofty concept of poetry, his sense of his vocation to be an intermediary between gods and men, the subtle equilibrium in his sense of poetry as an inspired higher knowledge *(sophia)* bestowed by the Muses, and the necessity for his own skill and art in the ordering and arranging of his words *(techne)*: everthing in Pindar's vision of poetry as a reconciliation between inspiration and art must have appealed to Ronsard. Then, too, Pindar was well aware of his own aristocratic birth and of the high station of many of his patrons. Though he wrote for a fee, he placed himself on the same level with the victor he celebrated in his songs; for as they achieved glory through inborn strength and acquired discipline, so he too, the poet, confirmed this glory in his compositions, shared in it, and passed it on to future generations.[9] This concept of glory was one which Ronsard admired and emulated. Though offensive to some of his contemporaries and hardly attractive to modern societies with their conventions of assumed modesty, Ronsard's cult of *la gloire* and his own role in confirming it was by no means alien to the feudal ideal still held by his own class. Without this ideal he could never have undertaken the mastery of humanistic studies, he would never have attempted the lofty flights of poetry which, though at times unsuccessful, led him to undoubted masterpieces.

One of the Pindaric odes of 1550 is dedicated to François de Carnavalet, Master of the Royal Stables.[10] Under the direction of this Breton nobleman Ronsard and his fellow students were trained in gentlemanly excercises. They were taught to jump and vault, the handling of arms, and horsemanship. Nor was their education in courtly manners neglected. The young poet could scarcely have found a more fitting subject for Pindaric praise than this Renaissance counterpart of the athletes and trainers of ancient Greece.

The ode is typically arranged in groups of three stanzas: strophe, antistrophe, and epode. Of these the first two have identical metric form: twenty seven-syllable lines with similar rhyme schemes made up of couplets, *rime croisée* and *rimes embrassée*. The epode, twelve lines of seven-syllable verse, has a different rhyme scheme, though composed of the same patterns.

Pindar's odes usually contain four traditional elements: praise of gods and men, including the victor, his family, and city; one or several myths related to the city or the games; moral lessons derived from the myth or the family history of the victor; and personal comments by the poet. These elements are all found in Ronsard's ode, though the gods are invoked only through their mediators, the Muses, daughters of Zeus.

The first stanza already contains many of the themes of Ronsard's ode. The poet speaks directly to Carnavalet, who is named in the second line. The power of verse to confer immortality is the theme of this address. The Muses, who alone can inspire the poet's song, are called down to show the place of Carnavalet in the poet's esteem. Ronsard mentions a promise to praise his patron, a promise which was long delayed, but is now fulfilled. The delay is a reminder of the fickleness of human life, and the fulfilling of the vow, together with an extra poem ("the interest on the debt") may actually have been true, or may have been inspired by Pindar.

The antistrophe continues the theme of the forgotten promise, which Time stirs the poet to fulfill. In an almost bantering way he decides to add the "interest." The remainder of the stanza dwells on the pleasure of conferring through poetry praise and immortality which alone conquers time. In a series of questions which form the epode, the poet asks which of Carnavalet's accomplishments he shall sing on his lyre: his knowledge and experience, his skill at training youth to follow the path of virtue, or his mastery of horsemanship which can teach the fieriest steed to become docile to the bit.

The last word ("bit") is the link with the myth of Bellerophon which Ronsard introduces in the next triad. In it he recounts the story of the gift of the bridle to Bellerophon, who, after vain efforts to tame the haughty "oldest son of Medusa" (Pegasus) has fallen into an exhausted sleep. Pallas Athene appears in a vision and presents her gift, the bridle, which immediately tames the animal. The antistrophe develops the exploits of Bellerophon on the winged horse, but in Pindaric style, seems to pass over this unhappy fate (which in fact it mentions), then moves quickly to the moral lesson taught by the myth: "The man who wishes to rise to heaven must rise by stages, not hurriedly." The theme of the training of horses returns in the epode, and with it the praise of Carnavalet, who is unsurpassed in teaching obedience and in preparing his animals to fight in the king's armies.

The final triad introduces briefly the illustrious ancestry of Carnavalet, his dual allegiance to Britainy (where his true name is Kernevenoy) and to France. His real ascendance, however, is from Virtue, and the poet will never tire of singing the praise of such men. The poem has gradually returned to the theme with which it began: Without the eloquence of poets, man dies without fame.

> But my honeyed eloquence
> Obeying my fingers' rule
> Mingled with the flute, will drive
> From thee oblivion.
> The nine holy maidens
> Are the guardians of glory,
> And my lute, made by them
> The high priest of their mysteries,
> Will spread upon thy progeny
> Some fragment of its grace
> Which grants thee immortality.

This ode is not great poetry, but it is obviously by a great poet. Few of the glaring defects of the other Pindaric odes are here, and few of the soaring lines. But many of Ronsard's finest qualities as an initiator of Hellenic poetry in French can be seen: his distinctive treatment of ancient metaphor; his skill in adapting myths particularly suited to his subject; and especially the ordering of all the elements into a coherent whole (hardly the "beau désordre" of the critics). All these are signs of his mastery of poetic feeling and technique in the sustained form.

IV *Horatian and Other Odes*

> Je volerai tout vif par l'univers
> Eternisant les champs où je demeure
> De mon renom engressés et couvers;
> Pour avoir joint les deux harpeurs divers
> Au dous babil de ma lire d'ivoire
> Se connoissans Vandômois par mes vers.[11]

The inspiration for Ronsard's earliest odes, and for most of the poems in the entire collection of 1550, was the Roman poet Horace. A glance at the critical edition is sufficient to reveal the debt that Ronsard owed to the entire body of Horace's poetry. The two poets seem to have many affinities. First among them, of course, was Horace's avowed aim in his odes to create a polished and elegant poetry and to adapt to the Latin language the subtle meters of the Greek lyric poets who flourished four or five centuries before him. Like Ronsard, too, he was writing for a society radically different from the Greece of Archilochus, Alcaeus, Sappho, and Pindar. Like his emulator, Horace was the heir to a tradition composed of several elements: ancient Greek, with all its diversity; the Alexandrian poets; and earlier poets writing in his own language. Horace, unlike Ronsard, does not seem to have been the self-appointed leader of a new school of poets. Rather he associated himself with the *neoteroi*, a group of poets who sought to lift poetry to a higher level of inspiration and refinement.

Though Horace wrote a number of odes denying his power to emulate Pindar (and showed considerable Pindaric inspiration in the process) he nonetheless revived some of the ancient Greek lore connected with the inspiration of the poet. Horace and his sophisticated readers certainly had no literal belief in the Muses as divinities, nor in the oracular gifts of the *vates*. Yet, when he sought to speak in the name of Rome and addressed the highest persons of the state, or sang of lofty ideals, the pudgy son of a freedman did not hesitate to don in his verse the trappings of the prophetic seer and spokesman of the gods, seized by divine fury. In doing so he gave elevation and gravity to his poetry and placed it beyond the ordinary and merely personal.

Horace's great concern with art and skill in addition to inspiration was a lifelong lesson to Ronsard. Both Pindar and Horace, in different ways, held this belief. The evidence of Horace's careful work, his exquisite marriage of form and substance, meaning, syntax, sound, and rhythm made him the poet most admired and followed by Ronsard throughout his career. If he, too, could create works of this sort, more lasting than monuments of bronze, he should win a place of immortal glory equal to that of the ancient poet. And he had no doubt he could.

Other deeper, less obvious similarities between the two poets appear as one becomes better acquainted with their poetry. One begins to realize, for example, that Horace's famous "nature" odes are not decorative landscapes. However subtle and attractive their details, they seem always to move with the moral theme of the life of man and its seasonal changes. Horace's invitations to banquets and to the pleasures of life are almost always coupled with a warning, explicit or implied, that each age has its pleasures, and that spring and summer are not eternal. In the end all mortals will go the way of pallid Death. The good things of life—friendship, good cheer, love—are to be enjoyed all the more because of the unknowable end which comes, sooner or later, to everyone. The swift flight of time, the cycles of seasons and of man, the taking of pleasure in its right place, the meeting of joy and pain and the final, inevitable end of it all, such are the themes of Horace's great poems. They are ageless themes, well worn by many of Horace's predecessors, and his debt to them was considerable. But, as has been said, he repaid his debt with interest. There is little cause for wonder that he became the ideal for some of Ronsard's loveliest poetry, and, at a deeper level, the perfect teacher of the art of setting old themes to new music which is ageless.[12]

It is in these odes celebrating the countryside, the work and sport of the fields, the seasons and their changes, friendship, love, wine, and the pleasure of life that Ronsard is best known and most congenial to modern readers. In them he shows his skill at taking the commonplaces of poetry, decorating and embellishing them in his own fashion, at once French, personal, and universal. He also shows, more clearly than in the Pindaric odes, his mastery of French verse forms, an easy handling of rhythm, a use of rhyme and run-on lines to give emphasis or to build a cadence, to evoke the sounds and sights of his native province, to inspire with new freshness the ageless theme of lovers. The reader, unaware of the poet's great erudition, has the impression that, in spite of the presence of gods and spirits, the poem is entirely French. Here Ronsard has succeeded in bringing into the mainstream of French poetry a whole current, bearing with it the riches of Greece, Rome, and Italy.

The ode *L'Avant-venu du Printemps*, not so well known as Ronsard's later poems on the coming of spring, nor so elegant as some of the light odes added in subsequent editions, is still a good example of Ronsard's mastery of the various elements of the lyric tradition. He has successfully combined the medieval spring song (the *reverdi*) with the timeless gods and spirits of the ancients, and with them added the note of philosophic speculation which the scenes evoke. The form, six-line stanzas composed of seven-syllable lines, is perfectly adapted to the rapid movement of the poem from one vignette to the next.

Each of the first three stanzas begins with an invocation, each addressed to a divine spirit or force. The rising notes of the first stanza are addressed to Taurus, both the zodiacal sign and Zeus who in the form of a bull seduced Europa. The poet calls upon Taurus to crash the barriers of heaven and open the gates of a new year. Next he calls upon an old man, guardian of the riches of the Earth, to open the door of Nature, who will decorate the fields with flowers and fruits. The third and longest invocation is addressed to the Nymphs, who are summoned to rise from the waters where they have been held captive by the ice and to decorate the banks of streams for lovers, so that the whole countryside may become a carpet scattered with blossoms, young, gay, painted with a thousand hues, victorious over Winter. This last invocation leads directly to an unbroken sentence of three stanzas, one example among many in the odes of Ronsard's mastery of the periodic sentence, each part clearly rising from the preceding, each building on the theme, rhythm, sounds, and word roots, each using syntactical bridges from one cadence to the next.

After the conquest of winter by the warmth of day, we see Jupiter planting the seeds of a new creation in the womb of his wife, thus saving the Cosmos from returning to a void. Other lesser agents of the divine force fulfill their functions as well. In a vivid tableau of the renewal of Nature by the force of Love, a passage reminiscent of the opening of Lucretius' great poem, we see the force of Love striking all living creatures.

Next Ronsard introduces miniature scenes from the drama of human life which correspond to the renewal of seasonal nature. In that age before technology life was still subject to the changes of seasons, and such scenes were a natural echo of the poetry of the ancients. Here we might have expected descriptions of rustic life, but instead there are stanzas devoted to a ship setting off for the Levant ("La charette vagabonde/Qui court sur le doz de l'onde"), and another stanza describing French soldiers preparing their pikes for an encounter with the Spanish infantry.

From the tableau of the soldiers setting up camp for the spring campaign Ronsard moves easily to the contrast between the present age of violence and the Golden Age, when spring was eternal and discord unknown. This blissful state was not allowed to continue by the jealous gods. The Golden Age vanished, and with it eternal spring, now followed by heat, wind, and ice. The pine from the valleys learned to sail the waves, the sound of armies is heard, of harnesses, of knives, of steel blades being hammered out on anvils:

> On ouit sonner les armes
> On ouit par les alarmes
> Rompre harnois et couteaux
> Et les lames acerées
> Sur les enclumes ferrées
> S'amollir sous les marteaux.

The repetion of words, dissonances and assonances, the reinforcement of key words by rhyme (*armes, alarmes; couteaux, marteaux; acerées, férrees*) and the repetition of the "r" as a harsh heroic sound are examples of Ronsard's mastery of capturing the sounds and discord of battle which so often recur in his work. For despite his scholar's longing for peace and his eloquent praise of its blessing, Ronsard never lost a nostalgia for a career at arms for which he was educated and to which his own class, the feudal aristocrary, was committed.

The poem ends with a falling away, a cadence hinting at other forms of destruction, destruction by poison and the shedding of blood. Its closing lines, in a Horatian succinctness unusual in Ronsard's more prolix verse, allude to the opening of Pandora's box of evils and the punishment of mortals by Jupiter's thunderbolt.

> Les maux du coffre sortirent
> Et les hauts rochers sentirent
> La foudre dessus leur flancs.

So the ode, which began on a note of rising expectation with Taurus breaking open the gates of a new season, closes with another opening in a distant, mythical past, the opening of the box of misfortunes. Spring, still the season of the ever-renewing work of divine creation through Nature and Love, is followed in the new age of violence by heat, wind, and ice. The coming of spring with its fruits and flowers is accompanied by the restless quest for riches by the merchant sailor and the clash of arms in dynastic wars, the fruit of greed and pride. We are reminded not so much of a line here or there from any ancient poets, but of the cyclic view of man's life, bound with seasons, so often presented in striking form in the seasonal poems of Horace. Spring is indeed lovely. but it is followed inevitably by other seasons.

Rich in their diversity of theme and lyric form as the Horatian odes are, they were not sufficient alone to fulfill the desire for great profusion and variety with Ronsard conceived of as the mark of true poetry. Many of the later odes of Horace are the poetry of a mature and successful man whose wisdom had come with years. His counsel of "everything in its season" was not always congenial to the young, hotblooded, sensual Ronsard. Other poets had sung of wine and love in more passionate strains; others had celebrated the delights of amorous dalliance, of Venus and her attendants, of Cupid, playful but treacherous child. For inspiration and example Ronsard tuned his lyre to the strains of Anacreon and his followers in the Greek Anthology; to the Roman elegiac poets Catullus, Propertius, Tibullus, and Ovid; and to their Italian imitators writing in Latin or Italian.

Many of these light odes or "odelettes" were added to the collection in 1552 or appeared in other works such as the *Bocage* and *Meslanges* of 1554–55. Since they are the most characteristic works of these later collections, they will be studied in the chapter devoted to these works. Here it is sufficient to note that these later odes provide the final balance to the entire collection; they are often the most familiar to the reader of Ronsard's lyric verse. These lighter odes have always been great favorites. The "rare and antique erudition" which is at times so apparent in the heroic verses seems absent from them. This of course is only an illusion, as will be seen. But they are graceful, melodious, and closer to the tradition of the French *chanson* and help to explain the partial acceptance of the entire collection of odes by the aristocratic and courtly public. This public and their favorite entertainer, Mellin de Saint-Gelais, did not accept the haughty new poet without making a protest which had serious affects on Ronsard and his poetry. One of the direct results of Ronsard's battle with the court and its poet was his greatest Pindaric ode, "Errans par les champs de la grace. . ."

V   *The Reception of the* Odes; *the* Ode à Michel de L'Hospital

Through the odes of 1550 runs the theme of the war on ignorance, sometimes expressed in mythological imagery, sometimes openly declared in scarcely veiled terms. No one doubted who represented the forces of ignorance in the newly declared war. Enough had been said and published by the brash young upstarts to stir up the defenders of the older French tradition which Ronsard and his friends professed to despise. The pretensions of these new arrivals, their use of strange foreign words (such as strophe, antistrophe, Patrie, etc.), of images brought literally from Greek and Latin, their mutual admiration—all were easy marks for an experienced courtier like the favorite of the day, Mellin de Saint-Gelais. Before the king and court he read excerpts from the *Odes,* emphasizing with voice and appropriate distortions the oddities of these pretentious novelties.

Ronsard was saved from the ridicule of the court and the continued enmity of Marot's followers by his principal patrons, Marguerite de France and her chancellor, Michel de L'Hospital. The latter, a distinguished jurist, humanist and neo-Latin poet, arranged an accommodation through the intervention of Jean de Morel, whose house in Paris was a gathering place for courtiers and humanists. In token of his gratitude Ronsard composed late in 1550 the last and greatest of his Pindaric odes, dedicated to L'Hospital and published in the revised and enlarged edition of the odes in 1552.

This splendid and ample poem, admired for its magnificent passages and criticized for its overuse of mythology and "disorder," is at last receiving its due recognition as one of Ronsard's masterpieces. It is indeed a striking example of his great poetic gifts: the development of a lofty theme through a series of episodes subtly linked together, the joining of narrative and descriptive passages by movement and melody, the capturing of the diversity of Homeric imagery and tone, the use of myth as ornament, narrative, and link between past and present—all these unite to demonstrate the vitality and subtlety of Ronsard's poetic vision. Since this poem has recently been the object of illuminating studies,[13] it seems appropriate here to present several passages from the ode in translation to give the reader some notion of the splendid poetry of the original.

As Professor Lapp notes in his recent study, Ronsard first introduces himself and his patron before proceeding to the body of the poem, which he develops in three major divisions. Here is the opening strophe (text of 1578):

> Wandering through the fields of Grace,
> Who colors my verses with her hues,
> On Dircean shores I gather up
> The choicest of the fairest flowers
> So that gathering them I might fashion
> With the labor of my hand
> The circle of this rounded crown
> Thrice twisted in a Theban ply
> To adorn in loftiest style the praise
> Of the happiest darling of the gods,
> Who from the skies brought back to earth
> The daughters born of Memory.

The opening lines, reminiscent of Pindar, show the poet gathering flowers of grace, the "flowers of rhetoric" or images, in order to combine them "with the labor of his hand"—not sheer disordered inspiration—into the threefold form of the Theban (Pindaric) crown. This crown, in the perfect form of roundness, will be the reward of L'Hospital, "the happiest darling of the gods" through whose efforts the Muses, the nine daughters of Zeus and Mnemosny (Memory), have been returned to earth.

The first part of the ode tells of the birth of the Muses and recounts their first visit to their father Zeus, who is being entertained below the sea in the palace of Ocean. Having "bound together with a wreath of violets and a chaplet of dainty flowers the gold of their unbound hair" Memory leads her children to the edge of the Indian Sea. They hesitate from fear: "These maidens, still innocent and ill-taught in efforts, Seeing the brow of those cruel waves, Were smitten with great fear: They all leaned backwards (So much were they dismayed) As one sees along some stream A reed bending beneath the wind. . ." Encouraged by a stirring speech by their mother and her own example, they follow her:

> They, then, beholding the path
> Of their mother, plummeting to sound
> The depths of the watery vastness,
> Opened by the strokes of her arms,
> With lowered head they sink below,
> Bending down their head and eyes
> Into the breast of the salty plains.
> The water, surging to the skies,
> Rumbles beneath them, gushes back,

> Hither and yon, curling up
> Into a thousand ringlets, swallows them
> Into the vast abyss of its throat.
>
> (Strophe 4)

This stanza is one of many in the ode in which Ronsard has conveyed a beautifully detailed picture animated with motion. Without having recourse to the much—condemned Homeric epithets he has conveyed in the concluding lines the organic unity of the sea and all living things.

After the arrival of the Muses at the palace of Ocean, where a great feast is in progress, they are welcomed by their father Zeus, and the central portion of the ode begins (Strophe 6). The Muses sing three songs, three myths of the gods, the first of which celebrates the founding of Athens and its naming in honor of Pallas Athene—an obvious tribute to learning and to Marguerite de France. The third myth, the most elaborate of the three, is the war of the giants and the gods of Olympus. This is the heart of the poem. Here Ronsard displays his talents to the fullest advantage. Again the myth has relevance to the patron for whom the poem is written, for the triumph of the gods is a type of the triumph of learning over ignorance. The third division of the ode (Strophe 11) begins with the request of the Muses for a favor from Zeus. The fairest of the group, Calliope, begins the request:

> Grant us, my father, she said,
> Father, she said, grant us
> That our immortal song
> In sweetness may surpass sweet sugar:
> Make us Princesses of the mountains,
> Of caves, of streams and of woods,
> And let the meadows and the fields
> Spring to life at our voice:
> Grant us further still
> The great crowd of divine bards,
> The Poets and Soothsayers,
> And the Prophets as our lot.
>
> (Strophe 11)

Ronsard, through the Muses, then expresses his concept of poetry and traces its future progress and decline, until at last it returns to earth in France under the aegis of Minerva-Marguerite and L'Hospital.

The entire ode is constructed with the utmost skill, and the numerous schematic and mythological devices, with their subtle echoes of Homer, Hesiod, and Pindar, link the various parts. The poem, which began with the poet and his patron, ends with them. The ode has come full circle. And it has the perfection of the circle, the Theban crown of the first stanza.

Thanks to the intervention of L'Hospital and Jean de Morel, Ronsard was saved from the ridicule of the court, though not from criticism, which continued for many years. After this Ronsard gradually abandoned his tone of aristocratic disdain. Saint-Gelais and the "Marotiques" responded to this spirit of reconciliation. Before long the former enemies were exchanging poetic compliments and dedications, and they seem to have been sincere. The final capitulation of the "Marotiques" was their own willingness to attempt the new genres advocated by Ronsard and du Bellay. In imitating Ronsard they acknowledged gracefully their acceptance of the new poetry.[14]

The reconciliation effected by Ronsard's patrons was just that; it was not total surrender of the old to the new. Carefully the friends of the poet suggested corrections and changes in his style: fewer strange words, obscure allusions, and bizarre images. Above all they recommended that he abandon exclusive claims on inspiration and learning. The direction of Ronsard's poetry in succeeding years is evidence that he profited from their advice.

CHAPTER 4

Les Amours de Pierre de Ronsard

I Ronsard and the Renaissance Sonnet Sequence

HAVING won acclaim as the French Pindar, the new Terpander, and the successor of Horace, Ronsard set about to add a crown of myrtle to the laurels bestowed on him by his admirers. His friends Baïf, Pontus de Tyard, Joachim du Bellay and Olivier de Magny had already published collections of sonnets dedicated to their ladies. All more or less followed the fairly pure Petrarchan tradition then fashionable in Italy. Ronsard was following this literary vogue when, in 1552, he published *Le Premier Livre des Amours de P. de Ronsard, Gentilhomme Vendosmois, ensemble le Cinqieme [Livre] des Odes.*

This collection and the subsequent *Continuation* and *Nouvelle Continuation des Amours,* the elegies, sonnets, and songs of later years, and his *Sonnets pour Hélène* have had a special appeal for his readers as well as an irresistible attraction for literary critics. Everyone who knows French literature is familiar with a half-dozen sonnets from the hundreds in the principal collections; on these sonnets and *chansons* much of Ronsard's reputation rests. "Mignonne, allon voir si la rose. . .; Marie, levez-vous, ma jeune paresseuse. . .; Comme on voit, sur la branche, au mois de mai la rose. . .; Quand tu seras bien vieille, le soir, à la chandelle. . ." These lines sing in the memory of all lovers of French poetry. From this handful of poems one can easily form an opinion of Ronsard as the singer of facile love, of young girls and roses, of a poet constantly urging them to enjoy, with him of course, the fleeting moment of youth, to pluck the rose before it fades. And this picture is by no means false. It is merely a detail from a much larger canvas. If one is content to know only the Ronsard of the anthologies, he will of course be quite satisfied with one rose from a bouquet containing a number of other flowers, even thorns and brambles. His rose will be perfect, but it will not have that rich diversity which is nature's, the diversity which Ronsard thought the mark of the true poet, the diversity which a reading of his collections amply confirms.

Ronsard was a poet of many loves. Some, whose names appear mysteriously disguised or abbreviated (Sinope, Genèvre, Marie, Jeanne, Marguerite) have remained enigmas. Others receive the dedication of entire collections: Cassandre Salviati, Marie from Bourgueil in Anjou, Hélène de Surgères.[1] To read and appreciate the poet's amatory verse it is not essential to know the biographical details concerning the women who may have inspired them. No doubt the knowledge of when and in what collection a poem first appeared can be of value, and the circumstances of the poem's composition may reveal something about it not otherwise apparent. What should remain foremost is the poem itself.

Ronsard himself has left a number of indications to confirm this interpretation of his attitude. From the first collected edition of 1560 till the posthumous edition of 1587 he constantly revised, added to collections, changed poems from one group to another, indifferent to their original dedication. Sonnets, odes and *chansons* move from *Amours I* (dedicated only in 1578 to Cassandre) to *Amours II* (dedicated, apparently, to Marie); poems from miscellaneous groups enter the sequences; sonnets are relegated to a collection with the revealing title of *Amours diverses*. If necessary, to make the poem appear suited for its new place, Ronsard will change names, months, and geography, though occasional lapses still betray the original intention to the practiced eye.

Two of Ronsard's friends wrote commentaries on the *Amours*. For the first book the humanist scholar Marc-Antoine de Muret provided an often elaborate gloss on classical and other references, elucidating neologisms and clarifying particularly recondite passages from mythology. This same function was assigned to the poet's young friend and latecomer to the "brigade," Remy Belleau, for the two *Continuations* (later *Amours II*). It is notable that in both cases the commentators, who enjoyed the collaboration of Ronsard, tell very little of the biography of the women most frequently mentioned, Cassandre and Marie. Occasionally they warn the reader that a certain poem is not addressed to one of these. For the editions of 1578, 1584, and 1587 Ronsard himself revised these commentaries, still attributed to Muret and Belleau. He is almost as indifferent as they appeared concerning the ladies of the collections.

Another indication of Ronsard's attitude toward his poetry is found in a letter to his friend and admirer, the poet and historian Charles de Sainte-Marthe. It is a letter written in pique by an aging poet and disillusioned lover in a tone which is anything but courtly and gallant. Hélène de Surgères, the senstive young lady who had inspired the last of Ronsard's sonnet sequences, had heard of preparations for their publication in the *Oeuvres* of 1578. Apparently she made objections to certain poems and, concerned about her chaste reputation, wrote to Sainte-Marthe, acting as Ronsard's literary agent in Paris. In answer Ronsard says: "... it is a great trial to serve a lady who has neither judgment nor understanding of our poetry, who does not know that poets, chiefly in small and insignificant trifles such as elegies, epigrammes and sonnets, observe neither order nor chronology. That is the concern of historians, who write everything in sequences." (".. . .c'est un grand malheur de servir une maitresse qui n'a jugement ny raison en nostre poësie, qui ne sçait pas que les poëttes, principallement en petis et menus fatras come elegies *[sic]*, epigrames et sonnetz, ne gardent ny ordre ny temps. C'est affaire aux historiagraphes qui escrivent tout de fil en equille.") Other disobliging things in the letter will be considered after the study of the sonnets.

A striking example of Ronsard's indifference to *Wahrheit* and complete preference for *Dichtung* can be found in his publication of the poems added to the *Continuations* in 1578. The new arrangement is called *Second Livre des Amours,* divided into two parts. The second, "Sur la mort de Marie," contains previously unpublished poems, apparently inspired by the same Marie from Bourgueil sung in the collections of 1555—56. Among these poems is the exquisite "Comme on voit, sur la branche, au mois de mai, la rose. . .," a sonnet which is justly chosen by almost every compiler of anthologies. Ever since Sainte-Beuve's *Tableau* critics have grown ecstatic over this lovely tribute to the dead "peasant girl" whom Ronsard had loved and celebrated years before. In 1922 Roger Sorg proved convincingly that almost every poem in Part II had been originally written "on command" of Henri III, striken with grief at the death of his youthful mistress Marie de Bourbon-Condé, Princesse de Clèves. By cleverly arranging the poems and placing them after the first part, Ronsard has incorporated them into a dyptich; like Petrarch's Laura, his Marie will have her poems of life and death.[2]

This discovery detracts in no way from the poetic merits of the sonnet; it continues to move us by all the qualities which might have come from a more "personal" inspiration. It has lost nothing of the elegiac sadness of a final tribute to youth and beauty. But this discovery should warn those who still insist on reading Renaissance "love poetry" as an intimate journal of the poet's life. Generally speaking it is true that most of the poems of this sort written by Ronsard "on commission" are inferior to his own "spontaneous" compositions. He himself confesses that he wrote best when he was moved by love. In love with whom? Often, we find, this is really not important.

Consciously or unconsciously, most readers, heirs of Romanticism, think of poetry and especially erotic poetry, as a deeply personal creation. It should be spontaneous, intimate, sincere. Though the collections of Renaissance verse which are attributed to esteem and to love of ladies may occasionally impress us with these qualities, they were really not requisites of such poetry at all. As a singer of love the poet was far more concerned with conveying a sense of admiration, suffering, desire, or whatever—whether feigned or real—in a form and manner both traditional and new. It is not so much his own private life that he evokes (though he may do so) or that of his lady, as that realm of lovers which, through his particular experience, he has entered. And once there, he is bound by the whole set of conventions which surrounded that realm.[3]

To many readers collections of Renaissance love poetry seem distressingly similar in their structure, form, and themes. And the place of convention in these verses is indeed frequently so controlling as to leave the poet little choice but to ring changes on well-worn tunes.

For centuries the French poet had expressed his amatory sentiments either in an idealized, courtly fashion—like some troubadour poetry—or else in a Gallic, lusty, and at times bawdy fashion. Fixed forms (*ballade, virelai, rondeau, chant royal*) were generally used, as well as the more popular and flexible *chanson.* With the beginnings of Italian influence in France, Petrarch and the Petrarchistic poets added several dimensions to the possibilities of expression as well as reinforcing the style of amorous imagery which can be traced back through the troubadours to the Roman elegiac poets (Catullus, Tibullus, Propertius, and Ovid) and ultimately to the Alexandrians.

With the triumph of humanism this classical heritage was added to the poet's possible choice of traditions. In the case of Ronsard the Greek and neo-Latin poets were special favorites. Thus Ronsard was particularly the heir of an almost embarrassingly rich heritage uniting French, Italian, neo-Latin, and classical poetry.

The French court and aristocratic society had, in the course of the sixteenth century, become increasingly Italianate. A society which professed to idealize the chivalric traditions of medieval France was in a sense ready to adopt the Neoplatonic worship of ideal beauty through the physical beauty of the lady. In both traditions, the courtly and the Neoplatonic, the lady was to be served, praised and adored by her suitor. If, as in the Petrarchan style, she was cold to his attentions, his expressions of devotion and suffering could be extravagant. An elaborate code of manners governed (ideally) the relationship of admirer and lady; and an equally elaborate set of images, based on ancient and medieval psychology, was used to describe every phase of the lover's adoration and suffering.

Ronsard's problem, like that of any poet of his time, was to compose amorous verse which somehow conformed to the traditions accepted by his society and the limited audience for which he chose to write. Since the older French forms of expression were bankrupt, according to the Pléiade, they turned to Italy, where the Petrarchistic tradition was already showing signs of exhaustion. But the mode was for things Italian, and Ronsard, for quite some time, bent his temperament to follow it. Personally it was often a sacrifice to fashion; for one whose temperament was sensual and impulsive, the courtly and especially the Petrarchan sublimation and self-abasement of a poetry which is essentially a series of compliments to the lady were at best poses, poses which must be adopted in accordance with literary and social convention. There are times when the pose can no longer be kept. As several scholars have noted, the satyr's pointed ears can be seen poking from beneath the cleric's cap.

To offset the heavy burden of the past, the tradition of centuries of amorous verse, the Pléiade poets had certain potential advantages. Not least of these was their language. Called by them "weak and poor" in comparison to Greek and Latin, the French of their time was nonetheless far richer than it had been in the past. Still unpruned by the merciless hands of Malherbe, the *précieux* of the salons, and the academicians, it was a tongue abounding in concrete, vivid, and picturesque words and sounds, evoking the countryside, provinces, and towns in which it was spoken. Lawyers, orators, and poets before the Pléiade had added lavishly from Latin to this popular base. The Pléiade poets and Montaigne had at their disposal an incomparable instrument for the creation of verse and prose remarkable for its plastic density and for its timbres redolent of the earth of France.

In the case of Ronsard his own talent and skill, together with omnivorous reading and the mastery of amorous verse from many traditions, combined with his sensual and impulsive nature conveyed by a sense of rhythm and sound, enabled him to use the resources of his native tongue to bring new life to the well-worn clichés of the poetry of love.

The use of a verse form new to France was another advantage exploited by the Pléiade. The sonnet, the form par excellence of Petrarch and his Italian emulators, had only recently been introduced into France by Marot and Saint-Gelais. Following the suggestion of Jacques Peletier du Mans the "Brigade" of Ronsard adopted it as their one modern poetic form. With its fixed number of lines, its set rhyme scheme in the octave and the possibility of many combinations in the two tercets, the sonnet structure was ideal for curbing a tendency to prolixity while at the same time allowing sufficient freedom for a variety of rhetorical patterns. Above all, it was Italian, it was fashionable, and it was new to France. The adaptation of the sonnet to a variety of themes and tones and the creation in this form of lasting masterpieces is one of the greatest achievements of Ronsard and his group. Once again we have the paradox of originality achieved through imitation.

II   Le Premier Livre des Amours.

In his preface to the *Odes* of 1550 Ronsard had scorned the frivolous courtiers whose only delight was in "a trifling Petrarchist sonnet, or some simpering love poem which drones on in the same key." Is his composition of a sonnet cycle predominantly Petrarchan in tone a confession of an earlier mistake, a sacrifice to court taste, an attempt to win over a larger public? Perhaps so. But it seems a mistake to view this first sonnet sequence as fitting the category condemned earlier by Ronsard.

There can be little doubt that one of the attractions of Cassandre Salviati, the daughter of a Florentine banker at the French court, was her name. For the pupil of Dorat and his "learned readers" this name evoked the unfortunate Trojan princess whose prophetic warnings went unheeded by her family. Here was a link with the world of Homer and Vergil which Ronsard did not fail to exploit. The heroic tone which he attempts in a number of the sonnets removes the collection, or at least a part of it, from the class of "simpering love poems."

A parallel to the *Odes,* the poems in *Amours I* often show similar techniques. Ronsard seeks to heighten the style by use of myth and by placing the conventional sequence of the events in the particular setting of his province; for myth and nature, by which the ancients often expressed the common experience of mankind, are at once individual and universal. As in the *Odes* the effects of mythology vary. At times Ronsard seems wilfully obscure, and the reader loses patience. At others Ronsard succeeds in heightening the dimensions and the evocative power of the poem.

It seems, in view of the entire sequence, that the frequent criticism of Ronsard's abusive use of mythology has been exaggerated. Even today when many educated readers have only a superficial acquaintance with ancient literature and the gods of Olympus, many of the poems can be read with few notes. The most frequent myths are generally familiar, and the heroes and gods are the central figures in the Homeric-Vergilian epics. One wonders if critics who repeat the accusations brought against Ronsard are reading selections, or whether they have an aversion to any use of mythology.

Perhaps two examples of the occurence of myth and legend will clarify the difference between abuse of learning and the use of ancient literature to add dimensions otherwise unattainable. Several sonnets might illustrate the pedantic; I have chosen Sonnet iv:

> I am not, my warrior-maid Cassandra,
>> Either a Myrmidon, or a soldier of the Dolopes
>> Nor that Archer whose lethal arrow
>> Killed thy brother and left thy city in ashes.

For my sake an armed camp from Aulis
    Sets not forth to make thee a slave
    And at the foot of thy ramparts are not seen
    A thousand ships come to carry thee away.
But surely I am that Corebus mad with love,
    Who for love of thee has his heart wounded,
    Though not by the hand of the Grecian Peneleus:
But by a hundred shafts which the victorious little Archer
    By a pathway hidden in my eyes,
    Without my knowing it, has struck into my heart.

(Laum IV, 8—9; Weber, 6; Cohen I, 4)

The reader is confronted with a whole cast of minor Homeric figures; unless he is fresh from a reading of Homer or Vergil they make no sense, and the sonnet remains a meaningless puzzle. The notes of Muret (or more modern editors) are necessary to clarify the significance of Myrmidons, Dolops; the Archer of 1.3 is Philoctetes; the reference to the Greeks besieging Troy is easier to grasp in 11.5–8; Corebus, to whom the poet compares himself, came to fight with the Trojans because of his love for Cassandra and was slain by Peneleus as he attempted to protect her from the victorious Greeks. The victorious little Archer is, of course, Cupid, the agent of love, whose arrows have found the way from the poet's eyes and struck his heart.

This compounding of overelaborate Homeric legend with the precious and mannered contrasts and comparisons of the two archers, is, despite its careful rhetorical structure, awkward and tedious. The poem might have pleased some of Ronsard's learned admirers and seems also to have survived the series of revisions and ruthless prunings to which he subjected these sonnets. One can realize that this is indeed, as Célimène told Alceste in Molière's comedy, "a completely new way of declaring love." But no amount of learning or poetic talent can save this poem—an extreme case, to be sure—from the accusation of being pedantic and tiresome.

Another example, among many, of Ronsard's use of myth can be found in the Sonnet "Or que Jupin. . ."

Now that Jove, pricked on by his seed
    Quafts in long drafts his accustomed fires
    And now with the heat of his fiery loins
    Implants his seed in Juno's humid womb:

> Now that the sea, now that the violence
>   Of winds gives way to great armed ships,
>   And now the bird within the tufted woods
>   Begins again her plaint against the Thracian:
> Now that the meadows, now that the flowers
>   With thousand, thousand, thousand hues
>   Paint so gaily the breast of the earth,
> Pensive and alone, to the most secret rocks
>   With muted heart I recount my woes
>   And through the woods, to hide my wound, I go.

(Laum. IV, 123–24; Weber, 100)

The opening lines (ll.1-4) are reminiscent of the spring ode from Book II *(Avant-venu du Printems);* both are supposedly derived in part from Vergil's *Georgics,* and in the sonnet there are also recollections of Horace. But the tone is entirely different from either. In his use of the myth of the fertilization of Earth by the Sky (Jupiter), Ronsard has transferred his sensual desire to a level of cosmic proportions. Here we are no longer in the typical Alexandrian or Petrarchan setting; this is not Venus at her dressing table surrounded by dainty Cupids. Nor is it the titillating Ovidian sensuality echoed by neo-Latin poets like Johannes Secundus. (There are many examples of both in *Amours I.)* The love act, frequently alluded to in conventional Petrarchistic love poetry by readily accepted figures or symbols (fires, death, faintings, the stolen heart, etc.) is here portrayed with the directness sometimes found in Greek poetry. At this early stage of his career, Ronsard makes an association of love and cosmic renewal connected with the cycle of seasonal fertility, an association which, in the seasonal *Hymnes* of 1563 and afterwards, becomes a controlling aspect of his vision of the fuller meaning of love.[5]

The next four lines (11.5–8), again reminiscent of the *Avant-venu* ode and with perhaps common sources, portray the winter winds giving way to spring; and again like the spring ode, the activity described is military, or evocative of past violence (in this case the crime of Thereus, the Thracian, is the cause of the complaint of the bird, the nightingale).

In this sonnet Ronsard has broken the usual structural division of 8:6 and joined the first tercet to the octave by the repetition of the introductory words "Or que. . ." with which each quatrain opens. The subject, likewise joining these lines to those above, is a scene of conventional springtime similar to the medieval *reverdi.* Here the meadows, such a common feature of medieval spring songs, may have the added significance of a pun on the married name of Cassandre, who in 1546, became *la dame du Pré* (meadow) a property near La Possonnière The "sein de la terre," often a cliché of the spring song, here evokes the "sein" (womb) of Juno .

In contrast to the spring tableaux of the preceding lines the final tercet sets off the poet, who alone of all creatures does not participate in this universal renewal. This conclusion, the most conventional and Petrarchan part of the sonnet (it is virtually translated from a well-known poem of Petrarch) is the closest link in sentiment and tone with the traditional pose of the lover. In the case of Petrarch himself (though rarely of his imitators) the introspection and inner withdrawal are real and essential to his nature. Wounded by love, he withdraws from society to a deserted natural setting to which he confides his inner feelings. Long before Ronsard, this had become a conventional pose, another tribute to the powers of the lady. And yet we should not be too hasty to place this in the realm of pure convention; for the poems of *Amours I,* and the *Odes* as well, abound in this kind of retreat into solitary landscapes, the countryside of Vendôme and Touraine. With Ronsard, a country man, this was natural; it was a lifelong custom. Who can say when literature ends and life begins?

Ronsard's mastery of the sonnet form is easily seen; he has clearly profited from his study of the Italians. Still working in the ten-syllable line traditional for lofty verse in French, he has organized the structure around the repetitive openings and the rhymes. These devices link the scenes and mark the major divisions. Within each section the opening pattern is repeated, though at different places in the lines, thus avoiding a rigid symmetry. The repetition also serves, as it frequently does in *Amours I,* to carry the movement forward. The doubling of the *or que* (11.5 and 9) gives the effect of an *accelerando* to the rhythm, and (1.9) builds to the climax of the scene with the insistent repetition of *mille* (1.10), which would otherwise be nothing but the weakest sort of padding. The movement slows (1.11), leading to the poet himself who, in contrast to the previous openings, is set off by "Seul, et pensif." The final tercet, the closing cadence, is thus the period to which the entire poem has been leading. Like many poems of the collection, it is composed of only one sentence in which each part builds from the preceding.

The use of classical learning and elaborate language does not succeed in removing the sonnets of *Amours I* from the realm of the Petrarchistic sequence. All of its conventional themes are here: The *innamoramento* in which the carefree poet, smitten by love through the eyes of the lady becomes a captive of her charms; adoration and praise of Cassandre's beauty, for which no comparison is too exotic, no hyperbole too farfetched, no setting too mannered or precious; the suffering of the poet, whose desire is rebuffed by the heartless fair; the evocation in absence of the lady's charms by the poet in solitary nature; and finally desire, at times sublimated to a vague ideal or attributed to the captivating beauty of Cassandre, at others a sensual longing often expressed indirectly through the veil of myth, or metamorphosis, or an erotic dream, occasionally expressed quite directly in an outburst of passion.

Ronsard, like most poets of his time, used the accepted symbols, which were in fact commonplaces of erotic language. Each age has its own. Today this conventional imagery seems quite artificial, in the modern, pejorative sense; in his own time it was admired by many for this very reason, artificial then having the sense of "done with art." Having accepted the conventions of the genre, he also accepted the language in which it was expressed, though rarely does he fall into the banal, the trite, the unpoetic. Yet all the conceits of the conventional pose appear: love as a war, as a poison, as a flame, as death-in-life; sighs as winds, tears as a stream; the antitheses and paradoxes of the captor captive, the prisoner of love, the captive heart—none are absent. The beauty of Cassandre, described in the most conventional fashion, receives lavish praise in terms of suns, gems, ivory, coral; her complexion appears a veritable garden of flowers. It is only when Ronsard's own peculiarly rich poetic gifts are apparent that he is superior to hundreds of others who have written in this style.

The sonnet "Soubz le cristal d'une argenteuse rive. . ." is a particularly happy example of Ronsard's use of conventional language and imagery to convey his compliments to the lady. Its music and rhythm defy translation, but perhaps some of its delicate charm can be conveyed in another language:

St. Mary's College Library

Beneath the crystal of a silvery bank,
In the month of April, a pearl I spied
Whose brightness so enraptured me
That to my speech there comes no other thought.
Its sphere was of such a natural white
And in its rays it glimmered fairer still.
Its sheen has not yet quenched my thirst.
Nor will it ever, no, ever, so long as I live.
A hundred, hundred times to fish it out
All stooping down I thrust my arm below,
Already happy, now I clasp it tight,
But for an Archer, who with his bow-tip
Face downwards plunging me beneath the lake,
Cheated my grasp of such sweet prey.

One characteristic of *Amours I* which seems particularly distinctive from many other collections is the expression of the poet's sensual nature. Some readers find that this sensuality is merely part of the pose; others find it personal and an essential trait of the collection. Even though many of the expressions in which Ronsard couches his sensuality are a part of the conventional language of compliment, it is still difficult to dismiss all of them as mere tributes to usage or literary devices to vary the tone. In addition to the language itself, rhythm, run-on lines, repetitions, cadences—all add to the impression of impetuous desire barely contained by custom and form. This is particularly evident in the text of 1552–53.[6]

The poet's sensuality may at times take the form of compliment. Many poems addressed to Cassandre (or to some other) are a praise of beauty. For this the poet chooses the most opulent of natural and artificial materials: silver and gold, rubies, pearls, alabaster, coral, unguents, exotic perfumes, silk and brocade. The sumptuous decorative settings of Renaissance paintings, the exquisite artifacts prized by the courtiers, the works of the first school of Fontainebleau all come to mind. Without the open-air settings in which Ronsard places his elaborately beautiful lady, the reader might well stifle in a suffocating hothouse. The highly refined imagery, the love of elegance, and the delight in the countryside are a part of Ronsard's many-sided nature which are in consonance with the tradition of the sonnet sequence and the tastes of his times.

Erotic desire, masked as compliment to the lady, as a myth or a metamorphosis, or, occasionally, expressed as raw passion, is by no means absent from the sonnets. The myth is often, in fact, a metamorphosis, or a series of them, in which the poet indirectly conveys his desire by allusions to the loves of the gods. Most frequently it is Jupiter whose amorous adventures the poet wishes to imitate. Another veil for sensual desire is the "songe amoureus" (the dream of love) in which the poet has a nocturnal vision of physical union with his lady.

Though strictly speaking neither a metamorphosis nor a dream of love, but rather a combination of the two conventions, the sonnet "Je voudrois estre Ixion & Tantale..." is typical of Ronsard's use of the gods to convey a desire which is at once burningly sensual, and at the same time couched in the hyperbole and distance of myth. Like many of the most sensual sonnets, it was added to the collection in 1553. And like them as well it was considerably softened in later editions. Here I follow the original text of 1553.

> I should wish to be Ixion and Tantallus
>   Upon the wheel, and in the streams below,
>   Could I at times press within my arms
> That beauty which equals that of angels,
> (If it were thus) all suffering decreed by fate
>   Were sweet to me, and I should pay no heed
>   Even though I were the feast of a vulture,
>   Even though I pushed the rock which falls.
> The mere fondling of her breast
>   Would transform the blackness of my destiny
>   To a fate far better than Asian princes',
> One kiss transform me to a demi-god,
>   And easing myself, thigh against thigh,
>   To one of those who feed upon Ambrosia.

Nothing could be more remote from Petrarch's introspection, nor from the precious compliments of society verse. Ronsard's use of myth to convey his own ardent temperment gives certain poems of *Amours I* a sense of youth and intensity never again found in his poetry. It is these qualities which are frequently overlooked and which deserve the attention of anyone who seeks to appreciate the creative genius of Ronsard who, though bound by conventions, used them to express his own poetic voice.

III *The* Continuations des Amours: *Marie*

After excursions into various kinds of short poems—lascivious, humorous, elegiac, discursive, epicurean, or descriptive—Ronsard returned to the composition of a sonnet sequence with the *Continuation des Amours de Pierre de Ronsard* (1555), followed within the year by another, more miscellaneous collection called *La Nouvelle Continuation . . .* (1556). Subsequently, by the deletion of a great many sonnets and some lyric pieces, the addition of others from the *Bocage* (1554) and the *Meslanges* (1555 and 1559), and of two long poems *(Elegie à Marie* and *Le Voyage de Tours)*, and a completely new arrangement, Ronsard created a second sonnet sequence to balance *Amours I* and named *Le Second Livre des Amours.* The creation of this new book of *Amours* is in fact one of the principal innovations of the first collected edition of 1560.

With further radical deletions of poems, equally radical revision of the text, and the addition of an entirely new second section entitled "Sur la Mort de Marie" the *Second Livre* of 1578 was ready to be "Dedicated to Marie" and is, of course, known as *Les Amours de Marie.*

The successive names under which Ronsard grouped these poems are indicative of certain changes in his poetic intention. Just as *Amours I* contained several poems having little or no connection with Cassandre, to which a number of later poems originally written for other occasions were added, so the *Continuations*, to a much more marked degree, began with many poems having only indirectly to do with love. A number of poems are letters to friends or patrons of which only a few mention the poet's new love. Marie herself figures directly in surprisingly few poems, and by name in even fewer. Cassandre continues to be mentioned and to receive the poet's attentions, as do a number of other "loves": another Marie, Jeanne, Marguerite, and so on. In each successive edition, beginning with the almost total re-creation of 1560, Ronsard deliberately sought to make Marie the center of the collection; removal of uncomplimentary poems, the mention of rivals, revisions of lines to include her name or the name of her village, and a change of tone gave the poems an intimate, rustic atmosphere. That, briefly, is the story of the gradual emergence of the *Amours de Marie* of 1578 and later editions.

Of Marie herself little is known. Remy Belleau, poet, scholar, and close friend of Ronsard, provided for the edition of 1560 a commentary which was reprinted in successive editions with revisions by himself or by Ronsard (1578, 1584, 1587). From it one may learn something of Marie's social station (implied as simple) and of several episodes in which both poets figure. As with Muret, the commentator is interested chiefly in the literary features of the work and not in the biographical. Much conjecture about the pine tree of Marie's village, Bourgueil in Anjou, has led to the interpretation of the pine is a *senhal* (a secret symbol used by the troubadours) for Marie's name, which would be either Pin or Dupin. All this is pure conjecture. Ronsard himself, in the texts of 1555—56, says that she is of lower social rank than Cassandre, that she is from Bourgueil in Anjou, that she is about fifteen years old, and that she has a sister Toinette (Antoinette), that he visited her on occasions, that she has given him cause for jealousy, and that for her he has changed his noble style into a lower one. In poems later omitted he implies that she was dull, stupid, and tiresome. Her physical portrait is almost entirely stylized, as are such adjectives as *honeste, humble,* and *gentille* (hardly the word for a "simple peasant.")

Much has been made of the contrast between *Amours I* and the *Continuations,* especially in respect to the style. Ronsard takes pains to discuss this change and attempts to explain it. The opening series of sonnets in the *Continuation,* in "vers heroiques" or Alexandrine lines, begins with poems addressed to friends. The first, to Pontus de Tyard, discusses criticisms of Ronsard's style. At first, he says, he was accused of being obscure and learned *(Odes* and *Amours I);* next *(Livret de Folastries)* of a style too low. No one will read the "style grave" and the public condemn the low style. The only solution is to laugh at all this. The last sonnet in the collection, addressed to Marie, also discusses style. The poet explains that because of his infatuation he has abandoned his "first grave style/Which was not destined to sing in such low fashion." If she had at least granted him her favors, he would have fewer regrets for this sacrifice.

The epilogue to the *Nouvelle Continuation,* placed in 1560 and afterwards as the preface to the entire book, is an *envoi* addressed to his book as it goes to face the public. In "A son Livre" Ronsard warns the book, his son, to beware of the sly critics awaiting it. Then follows a long anti-Petrarchan passage defending the poet's inconstancy in love; it is heavy with misogynistic arguments recounting in true medieval fashion the wiles of women. Then Ronsard turns to his new style:

So, if anyone come to reproach me
That no longer am I so grave in my verse
As at first, when Pindaric humor
Swelled with windy words my grandiloquent speech,
Tell him that loves are not whispered about
In lofty serious verse, but rather in a fine low style
Popular and pleasing, as Tibullus wrote,
The ingenious Ovid, and the learned Catullus:
The son of Venus hates those ostentations.
For him it suffices to sing his praises truly
Without bombast or paint, in a dainty sweet style
Flowing in soft sounds like a smooth running stream. . .

This preoccupation with style, and the attribution of its changes to a love affair, reveal Ronsard's greater concern with public appraisal of his work and an effort to bring his "fine low style," developed from the light odes of 1550 through those of the *Bocage* and *Meslanges,* into the realm of the Petrarchistic sonnet sequence. The lighter touch, the banishing of obvious erudition, the "rustic" setting in an Angevin village are all consonant with his poetic practice of 1553–56, the years in which he was most under the spell of the Alexandrian Greeks and their Latin followers. Ronsard's efforts to perfect what must really be called a "middle style" coincided with an unsettled approach to the sonnet sequence. His compromises are obvious: the constant deletions, rearrangements, and revisions show his ceaseless attempts to give unity through style to a collection which, in the original text, was anything but unified in tone or structure.

By ignoring the continuity with *Amours I* implied in the original titles and by focusing attention on style one may indeed see the contrast between the earlier sequence and these new poems. One can point to the "natural" style, the charming rustic setting, the vignettes of provincial life, the easy sensual banter, the lack of heavy erudition. In a sense this appraisal is justified, but only if one omits possibly two-thirds of the poems (many were suppressed in 1578). The usual appraisal does actually fit the best-known of the anthology pieces: "Mignonne, leves-vous, vous estes paresseuse" (a delightful poem, but hardly typical of the collection); "Je vous envoye un bouquet de ma main . . ." (suppressed in 1578); "Je mourois de plaisir voyant par les bocages . . .;" "Je veux lire en trois jour l'Iliade d'Homere . . ." (likewise suppressed in 1578, possibly because it is addressed to

Cassandre); from the *Nouvelle Continuation* the songs "Bon jour mon cueur, bon jour ma doulce vie . . .;" Belle & jeune fleur de quinze ans . . .;" "Ma maitresse est toute angelette . . . ." All are known and held typical. But the collections in their entirety are far from the rustic, natural, spontaneous, and popular. In fact the "beau stile bas" is not really "bas" but decidedly "beau."

The "Elegie à Jean de Morel," which dedicates the *Nouvelle Continuation* to Ronsard's friend and protector, is quite as interesting as the better-known epilogue "A son Livre"; in the original arrangement the two poems frame the collection. After a learned opening, taken from an episode of the *Argonautica,* whose purpose is to illustrate the hidden value of small things, Ronsard dedicates his small work to his friend. Then, in a passage which is, in effect, his apology for this short work and the answer to those who have blamed him for abandoning his projected epic, Ronsard continues:

> Now this small effort which I dedicate to thee
> Is small in appearance, I know full well,
> But truly it is not so small as one thinks:
> Perhaps its value is more than the bulky show
> Of those swollen tomes, which within have naught
> But frowning verses, great windy words,
> Puffed up, and masked, where naught is found
> Save the arrogant mumble of a pretentious work.

Following several lines on the collapse of pretentious and ill-constructed buildings, Ronsard returns to his apology:

> I fully grant thee that the River Seine
> Has a grand and lengthy course, but ever it sweeps
> With it mud, and its twisting folds,
> Never a moment clean, are always full of muck.
> A small rivulet has always a pure stream;
> And so the butterfly and the gentle bee
> Go there to draw their water, not to those torrents
> That, thundering with great noise, rush through rocks.
> Fair little sonnets, fair little songs
> Little verses made with care are the flowers of the Graces
> The [nine] Sisters, and Apollo, who deign not to love
> Those who sing a song as great as the sea
> Without shore nor bed, bristling with tempests,
> Never sleeping in tranquility and calm.

Ronsard, who was writing his *Hymnes* at the same time as the *Continuations,* had turned again to an early favorite, the Alexandrian poet Callimachus. According to tradition, he had been the leader of the school of poets who preferred the small, exquisitely wrought work to the large, rambling, and pretentious epic. In Callimachus and his followers, both Greek and Latin, Ronsard found the justification for devoting his talents to the creation of the shorter works distinguished by fine detail and consummate craftsmanship. Thus, what is referred to in the two poems mentioned above as a "stile bas," "populaire & plaisant" is decidedly a *Beau stile bas.* One has only to recall the Latin authors mentioned in "A son Livre" and the adjectives describing them to recognize that Ronsard is certainly not abandoning a highly stylized work: Tibullus, the ingenious Ovid, and learned Catullus. The whole of the *Amours II* is prefaced by Belleau's commentary which ends with a quotation from Propertius, hardly a popular poet. In both poems Ronsard describes this new style as "mignard et dous," a key term in the collection itself. Finally the image of the clear little stream, which may derive from several of the poets mentioned in "A son Livre" is found likewise in both poems. Though it is not mentioned in the notes of the critical edition, it seems to me that the source of the passage from the *Elegie* contrasting the muddy river and the limpid stream comes from the end of Callimachus' *Hymn to Apollo,* a work often imitated by Ronsard. All the evidence points to the clear indication that Ronsard, while he certainly intended his poetry to be more "populaire," also had no intention of adopting the vapid and artless ditties of the court poets as his model.

If Ronsard has found his new style, he has not yet found a way to reconcile his own temperament and expression within the traditional Petrarchistic sequence. The hybrid nature of the *Continuations,* particularly of the second collection, reveal this uneasy attempt to change the pattern and escape from a convention which was inadequate.[7] The *Nouvelle Continuation*, in fact, is not a sonnet sequence at all; few poems deal with the poet's feeling for Marie, though some treat generally of love. In form many poems are odes, odelettes, and even the formerly despised *chanson* for which Ronsard could find models not only in Petrarch and the neo-Latins but in the Greek Anthology. Rather than a sonnet sequence, this last collection seems more like the *Bocage* and *Meslanges* with its descriptive *blasons* of plants and animals, and the final group of poems addressed to friends and patrons.[8] The removal of these miscellaneous poems to other groups in 1560 was clearly necessary before Ronsard could make of this mixture a book of *Amours.*

In the case of the sonnets and lyric pieces retained in *Amours II* for the collected edition of 1578 Ronsard took great care to make a number of revisions in the text; his motives, in some instances, may have been similar to those which prompted revisions of the odes and *Amours I.* In revising *Amours II,* however, he was far more concerned with giving unity to a collection which had obviously lacked it, and, insofar as possible, to contrast the second "rustic" love with the first, "noble" one. A clear, if not altogether typical, example of this revision may be seen in the two versions of the following sonnet. In this case all the significant changes were made at once for the 1578 text and retained in 1584 and 1587: (For the sake of emphasis I have underscored the revisions of the 1578 text.)

    I.   Text of 1555:

> Douce, belle, gentille, & bien fleurente rose,
> Que tu es a bon droit à Venus consacrée,
> Ta delicate odeur hommes & Dieus recrée,
> Et bref, Rose, tu es belle sur toute chose.
>
> La Grace pour son chef un chappellet compose
> De ta feuille, & tousjours sa gorge en est parée,
> Et mille fois le jour la gaye Cytherée
> De ton eau, pour son fard, sa belle joue arrose.
>
> Hé Dieu, que je suis aise alors que je te voi
> Esclorre au point du jour sur l'espine à recoy,
> Dedans quelque jardin pres d'un bois solitere.
>
> De toi les Nymphes ont les coudes & le sein:
> De toi l'Aurore emprunte & sa jou, & sa main,
> Et son teint celle-la qui d'Amour est la mere.[9]

    II.   Text of 1578–87:

> Douce, belle, *amoureuse,* et bien-fleurante Rose,
> Que tu es a bon droit *aux amours* consacrée!
> Ta delicate odeur hommes et Dieux recrée,
> Et bref, Rose, tu es belle sur toute chose.

Marie, pour son chef *un beau bouquet* compose
De ta feuille, et tousjours *sa teste* en est parée:
Tousjours ceste Angevine, unique Cytherée
Du parfum de ton eau *sa jeune face* arrose.

Ha Dieu, que je suis aise alors que je te voy
Esclore au point du jour sur l'espine à recoy,
Aux jardins de Bourgueil pres d'*une eau* solitaire!

De toy les Nymphes ont les coudes et le sein,
De toy l'Aurore emprunte et sa joue, et sa main,
Et son teint *la beauté qu'on adore en Cythere.*

An examination of the variants of 1578ff. reveals the change of tone achieved by the replacing of phrases and adjectives. In the first quatrain *gentille* (l.1) is replaced by *amoureuse,* a more appropriate adjective in this sonnet-*blason* linking the rose to the goddess of love and, in the revision, to Marie. Further, the deletion of *gentille,* with its overtones of aristocratic gentility, suits Ronsard's purpose in making the sonnet appear to have been dedicated to his village sweetheart of 1555. The sound of the new word also enriches the *-eur* words: *fleurante* and *odeur.* In l.2 à *Venus* is removed and, in its place, *aux amours* gives a more general and far less classical tone; one can already see Ronsard's intention to eradicate the traces of Anacreontic style. The new phrase also adds an echo of the *amoureuse* of l.1. Instead of a Hellenistic personification of a Grace (Charité), the name *Marie* opens the second quatrain (l.5). The archaic but charming *chapellet* is sacrificed for the more ordinary *bouquet,* a word reinforced with *beau,* both for the sake of rhythm and because it is too vague. The alliteration thus introduced compensates for the one lost in *chef–chapellet.* Ronsard adds a modest note more fitting for his country lass by the word *teste* which replaces the *gorge* (de Venus) (l.6). Once again the revision adds an alliteration. In the following line (l.7) only the last word *Cytherée* remains of the original text, and in its new context it has changed function to stand in apposition with Marie *(ceste Angevine),* another specific reference to the poet's love and her province. The banal expression *mille fois* (which is thus deleted) is certainly no loss. Again Ronsard removes traces of the Alexandrian tone of the original text by banishing Venus (la gaye Cytherée). Not only is Cytherea herself removed from the picture, but the line describing her *toilette* (l.8) is happily rewritten to add a note of freshness and naturalness almost totally absent from the original. By removing the *fard* (l.8), and recalling the *odeur* (l.3) with the word *parfum* and retaining *de ton eau* as a dependent phrase, Ronsard gives a charming picture of the young girl and the flower. The girl herself is evoked by the new phrase *sa jeune face,* more appropriate for youth than the pretty cheek of the goddess. Thus the removal of the *fard* with its connotation of cosmetics and artificiality again alters the tone. One last revision and the transformation is complete: the vague expression *Dedans quelque jardin* becomes *Aux jardins de Bourgueil* (l.11), the village of Marie on the banks of the Loire never mentioned once in the original texts of the *Continuation.* The final master touch, the *eau solitaire* echoes the *eau* of l.8 and avoids a clash in sound with the word *Bourgueil.* In all these changes one can see a master poet at work. The revisions, in every case, seem to me unusually appropriate. Unlike a number of those in the texts of *Amours I* they have not eradicated one value and replaced it by a generality; they have replaced one tone by another and added to the musical quality of the verse.

IV Le Voyage de Tours

In the *OEuvres* of 1560 an attractive and curious poem is added in the very center of the collection of sonnets and songs: "Le Voyage de Tours, ou Les Amoureus Thoinet et Perrot," a pastoral poem in 346 Alexandrine verses. Ronsard's friend Jean-Antoine de Baïf, who had already composed unpublished eclogues, accompanied him to a country wedding on the island of Saint-Cosme near Tours, where Ronsard would soon be named prior. The two friends set out from La Possonnière on a fine spring day:

> It was the season when amorous Flora
> Made the buds of flowers open for her friend
> Through the meadows dappled with enamelled blooms
> As many in color as the great bow of heaven.
> Then the butterflies and the blond honeybees,
> Then some with beaks full, some with thighs laden,
> Wander through gardens, and the tiny birds
> Flitting through the woods from branch to branch
> Fill up their beaks, and in the green wood
> Take care, like us, of their future race.

(ll. 13-22)

The two "shepherds" (Thoinet-Baïf and Perrot-Ronsard) pass through the forest of Gastine, spend the night with friends, and arrive the next day to find the wedding guests gathered on the island. Among them are Francine, the love of Baïf, and Marion, Ronsard's Marie. First Thoinet declares his love to Francine in a speech full of reminiscences of their past meetings (ll. 47–188). One passage is remarkably similar in mood and in its view of love and memory, of past and present, to the beautiful elegy Ronsard will compose for Cassandre in 1569 ("L'absence, ny l'oubly ... "). Now, Thoinet declares, he is no less overcome. by love for Francine than when he first saw her:

> Six years have passed, and yet in my ear
> Still I hear the sound of thy matchless voice
> Which won my heart, still I remember
> Thy bright red mouth, thy golden hair,
> Thy hand, and thine eyes; and if passing time
> Has since stolen some part of their grace
> Yet am I no less charmed by thee
> Than on the Clain the day I saw thee
> Surpass in beauty every shepherdess
> Which the young shepherds held most fair.
> For I have no care for what thou art,
> But for what thou wast, so much the darts of love
> Have graven thee in me, even in such wise
> That as thou wast, so I bear thee in my heart.

(ll. 81–94)

Just as Perrot prepares to make his speech to Marion, her mother appears and whisks her away on a boat. As it leaves Perrot addresses to the boat a "convoy," a series of elaborate wishes to accompany his beloved on her way home. As often happens with Ronsard his desire is expressed in a metamorphosis. Here, after the "convoy" he wishes to become transformed into a river-god to bear the boat; then, once Marion is on shore, to resume human form and surprise her as she climbs from the reedy bank. Next he thinks of pleasing her with simple presents, and then of building a fanciful bower. This bower is beautifully and lavishly described as Perrot thinks of the periwinkle, lavender, wild mint, water lilies, and reeds which he will gather for it. There in this retreat he will pipe away his cares and drink the wine of

Anjou. (ll. 261–74). Two rustic musicians with rebeck and bagpipe will sing of his love in spite of Marion's disdain.

But this idyllic life is only a dream fantasy (as so much of *Amours II* seems to be), and the two poets return on their skiff to the Vendôme, and to their daily occupations.

This poem, so redolent of Touraine and Anjou, bears many traces of Ronsard's renewed interest in the Alexandrian bucolic poet Theocritus, and the later Latin writers of eclogues. Once again, Ronsard, in search of a way to round out his collection of love poems and to find a means of expressing his love of love in a new way unhampered by the conventions of the Renaissance compliment-hyperbole, has found his inspiration and guide from the labyrinth in his Greek poets. The vision of love as simple fulfillment in a natural setting (however artful its portrayal) is one of Ronsard's richest and happiest poetic resolutions of the dilemma of the Renaissance love poem.

CHAPTER 5

The Master Musician

I *Ronsard's Collections of Lyric Verse (1552–1559)*

O NE of the most attractive features of the *Odes* of 1550 is the number of fairly short lyric pieces. Whether inspired by Anacreon
or the Greek Anthology, the Alexandrian poets, by Horace or the
neo-Latin poets, these poems have certain qualities in common which
mark them as a distinct group. They have only a few stanzas, usually
three to five. They have short lines, varying from three to eight
syllables, with lines of seven or eight syllables predominating. Their
rhythm is quite flexible, and their sound patterns, though at times
subtle, are euphonious. All these are distinctly musical qualities,
qualities which must have attracted Ronsard to the poems in Greek and
Latin which are his models, qualities which he attempted to render in
his own poems. As we know, the odes were from the beginning set to
music by the outstanding composers of the Renaissance and have more
recently attracted composers such as Debussy, Ravel, Milhaud, and
Poulenc.

Though the largest number of Ronsard's lyric poems date from the
first decade of his career he never ceased composing short poems either
in stanzaic form or in non-stanzaic forms, though inspired by the same
poets. The additions to the *Odes* (1552, 1555) and the odes and
odelettes of other collections were eventually joined to those published
in 1550. All these were originally designed to be sung. Other lyric
poems appear under different titles, but are really similar in tone and
often in form: the *voeux* based on the short vow made to a god; the
epitaph, often in lyric form; the *chanson,* the native French form so
similar to many of the light odes; and the short descriptive piece known
in French as the *blason.* Taken all together these poems form one of the
richest and most varied collections of lyric verse in French, and a small

number, together with certain sonnets, have remained the most admired and accessible part of Ronsard's vast poetic creation.

If Ronsard's composition of new poems in lyric form after 1556 is notably reduced, his concern with the form remained undiminished. The care with which odes, *chansons, gaités,* and short epitaphs were revised for each of his major collected editions is proof of his keen interest in these poems. In some cases these revisions are a complete rewriting of the poem, a re-creation. The same infinite pains which can be seen in his revisions of other forms can be observed in his treatment of the short lyric: removal of obscure words, references, ambiguities, and obsolete words; removal of awkward transitions or redundant passages; occasional substitution of a more general, abstract word for an older, more vivid one; deletion of unharmonious elements; and the effort to compensate for the loss of one poetic value by the addition of another. This process of re-creation, begun in 1552, continued until the last year of the poet's life.[1]

Ronsard published five collections containing most of his lyric verse between 1550 and 1560. First were the *Odes* (1550, 1552, and 1555) whose longer poems have already been studied. In 1553, perhaps in a reaction against the Petrarchan conventions of the *Amours,* he published anonymously his *Livret de Folastries,* a collection of erotic poems rather free in tone and content. Some are popular and Gallic in their rustic and earthy language, while the last group is based on Greek originals. This book was never again published during Ronsard's lifetime, though some of the less offensive poems were moved to other collections under the title *gaités.* The *Bocage* of 1554 is, as its title based on the *Silvae* of Statius implies, a group of various kinds of shorter poems, with several longer poems mixed among them. The *Meslanges* of the following year is really the same kind of collection. In addition to these two books of predominately lyric verse, the *Continuations des Amours* (1555–56) contain a number of odes, odelettes, and *chansons* later incorporated into the *Odes.*

The hundreds of poems which compose these collections require six volumes in the critical edition. Faced with such an *embarras de richesse* I have chosen several poems illustrative of the great variety of Ronsard's lyric style. In general such deservedly famous poems as "Mignonne, allon voir si la rose . . .," "Bon jour, mon coeur . . ., "and" Bel aubepine . . ." have been omitted, not because they are unrepresentative or inferior, but because they have been reprinted so many times and are the subject of so many studies and *explications de texte.*

The odes, odelettes, *chansons* and other lyrics, whose most attractive qualities are musical, defy translation, since they depend for their effect on rhythm and sound joined to and reinforcing meaning. While to an extent this is true of all poetry, it is particularly noteworthy in these poems. Anyone who wishes to appreciate them should hear the poems read or sung in French. The translations given in this chapter are meant only as a guide to the French text of Ronsard. In choosing from the various versions of the poems published by Ronsard I have selected the one which in my own judgment is the best and have indicated the date of the text in each case.

II *Anacreontic Songs*

In 1554 the scholar-printer Henri Estienne published his edition of the poems attributed to Anacreon. Before that time, however, Ronsard, a friend of Estienne's, had had access to the poems attributed to the Greek lyric poet. Ronsard's versions of these poems are considered much freer and on the whole more original and more musical than those published by his young friend Remy Belleau, as a comparison of their versions of the same poem will reveal.[2]

Evidence of Ronsard's interest in the Anacreontic poems can be found in the early odes, and it became quite pronounced in the *Bocage* and the *Meslanges.* The three *Odelettes à Corydon* of the *Bocage* (Laum. VI, 102–7), later transferred to the second book of odes, are fine examples of Ronsard's adaptation of the Greek poems and his transformation of the ancient poems into a French form which still retains the spirit of the Greek banquet song. Corydon, a classical name for shepherd or a cupbearer, is urged in the first poem to fill the cup so that the young poet may forget cares, old age, and death. In the second, which will be studied below, the same mood prevails, but with the introduction of commonplaces on the coming of death. The third, often printed in anthologies, shows Ronsard combining several Anacreontic poems with Horatian themes to produce a charming and humorous picture of the young humanist, tired of his studies in the *Phemonena* of Aratus, preparing to leave his books for a picnic in the country. Here is a translation of the first stanza of this poem (text of 1554):

My head is splitting
From too much studying
Aratus's Phemonena:
It's time to frolic,
To play in the fields.
Ye Gods! who'ld praise
Those, glued to a book,
Who've no concern to live.

The sprightly seven-syllable lines, rhyming couplets, run-on verses, and broken rhythms set the mood for the delightful picnic of wine—with the bottle stopped by grape leaves and cooled in a spring—apricots, melons, strawberries and cream—all to be enjoyed beside some cool stream or in a cave nearby.

The second poem to Corydon follows fairly closely the Anacreontic poem. The following translation is based on the text of 1554:

To drink upon the tender grass
I'll stretch beneath a Laurel.
Let Cupid, with a tiny bit
Of linen or of hempcloth,
Tuck up his light robe
And, almost nude, pour wine.

The uncertain life of man
Rolls ceaselessly on as
The waves roll on the shore,
And after our last hour
Our remains in the bier
Are naught but some small bones.

Let none, according to the custom,
Perfume my tomb with incense
Nor spread sweet odors there;
But while I have life
I'll have sweet scents
And crown myself with flowers.

Corydon, go fetch my girl
Before the pallid Fates
Send me to eternal nights:
I'll drink the brimming cup
And by her side banish the care
Of misery and anguish.

Like Jacques Amyot, the translator of Plutarch's biographies and moral essays so much admired by Montaigne, Ronsard has "naturalized" the Greek poem and made it, in a way, quite French without losing the essentially pagan and ancient spirit of the original. The myrtles and lotus leaves of the original have been replaced by a laurel under which the poet "stretches out on tender grass," a detail not found in the Greek. The Hellenic Cupid is dressed "in a tunic tied over his neck with a papyrus-ribbon," but Ronsard's diety has his gown tucked up to his waist with a bit of flax or linen and hemp. In his poem Ronsard follows the second stanza of the Greek fairly closely, though he replaces the image of the chariot wheel by the verb *rouler* (to roll) and use the *topos* of the waters of the streams and the ceaseless waves of the ocean to represent the life of man and its ebbing with time. The pagan note is retained in the third stanza, again a close version of the original in which the tomb and the unguents or perfumes and the flowers of the funeral offering are retained, though scarcely French. Also retained is the poet's chaplet of flowers, familiar in France from popular festivals, though perhaps not in the context of this poem. The final stanza is more vivid than the original, introducing the "Parque blesmie," the "eternelles nuits," and the "miserables ennuis" not mentioned in the Greek poem, though certainly implied. The use of these adjectives in French compensates for the weaker and shorter verbs of the French and shows Ronsard's fine sense of the Greek and the limits and possibilities of his own language.

This charming musical composition was, in my opinion, spoiled by Ronsard's revision of 1584-87. In this version the last stanza reads:

> I'll make of myself
> My heir for my contentment.
> I'll not live for others.
> Foolish the Pelican who bleeds
> For his young, and foolish he
> Who for his own is wracked.

The harsh egotistical tone, absent in the first version, introduces a discordant note which clashes unpleasantly with the previous stanzas. The image of the pelican feeding its young from its wounded breast, even though this selfless act is mentioned only to be coarsely ridiculed, is out of place in such a poem. We can only wonder what prompted Ronsard to sacrifice perhaps the finest stanza of his poem for this bitter and poetically inferior conclusion. This is only one instance of hundreds in which the complicated process of Ronsard's revisions allows us to see the poet at work but leaves us no clue as to the motives which may have prompted his changes.

The image of death, shown in so many guises, which haunts many of Ronsard's poems, is often present in Anacreontic verse as well, like the skeleton at a banquet. In the Greek songs this picture has little of the gripping violence of the grim reaper which occasionally appears in other ancient literature, nor does it show the stark and hideous realism which Ronsard's age seems to have inherited from the late Middle Ages. This Christian medieval portrayal of death mingles, in the great *Hymne de la Mort* of 1555, with pagan images and appears occasionally in some of the "baroque" poems of Ronsard's last days. In spite of its theme of old age and death, the poem "Ma douce jouvence est passee . . ." is certainly not grim, and one may be surprised to see this version of the Greek song discussed as though it were a confessional self-portrait of Ronsard.[3] The following translation is based on the text of the *Odes* of 1555 (IV, xviii):

> My sweet youth has passed away,
> My early strength is broken,
> My teeth turned black, my hair turned white,
> My muscles weakened, and my veins,
> In my cold body, are full of naught
> But rusty water, in place of blood.
>
> Farewell, my Lyre, farewell maidens,
> Once my sweet playmates.
> Farewell, I feel my end draw near.
> No pastime of my youthful days
> Goes with me into my old age
> Save the fireside, the bed, and wine.
>
> My head is now full weighted down
> With many years, and sickness
> From every side bites at me:
> And whether I go or whether I linger
> Ever at my back I look
> To see if death is coming,

> Who must, I feel, at any hour
> Take me down below where dwells
> Some aweful Pluto, who keeps
> For all who come a yawning cave
> Where all may enter easily
> But whence no one returns.

Perhaps the choice of such a poem for his version may tell us something of Ronsard in 1555, but it can hardly be considered as a personal portrait. It is rather a subtle musical adaptation of the Greek of the Anthology showing the other side of the picture of pleasure so frequently associated with Anacreontic verse.

III *The Songs of Marullus*

One of Ronsard's favorite poets, the inspirer of both the light erotic *chansons* of the *Nouvelle Continuation* and of many of the serious *Hymnes,* was Michael Marullus. A Byzantine by birth, Marullus lived most of his life in Italy, where he died in April 1500. Like many authors of the time he wrote exclusively in Latin. This neo-Latin literature of the Renaissance, so little known and read today, was not merely a pale reflection of its ancient predecessor. At their best, the poets who wrote in Latin at this time were the rivals of all but the most eminent of the ancient Romans. In the light epigrams and the hymns of Marullus, the French poets recognized the same qualities they cherished most in ancient poetry. Like Ludovico Ariosto, a personal friend of Marullus, Ronsard wrote for his favorite neo-Latin poet a moving epitaph, "Dites bas de bonnes paroles. . ." which he published in the *Bocage* of 1554. Here are the opening stanzas translated from the first version of the text:

> Epitaph of Michael Marullus . . .

> Whisper low gentle words,
> Muses, and with my songs
> Tune softly the sounds
> Of your Lutes and Viols.

> Here is the tomb of Marullus:
> Pray that ever upon it
> Sweet manna, sweet honey
> And sweet dew from heaven may fall.

> I err, this is not Marullus's tomb,
> This tomb has naught of him
> But the empty letters of his name:
> He lives with Tibullus below,
>
> Upon the Ellysian shores,
> And beneath the green myrtle's shade,
> To murmuring streams he sings his verse
> Among the choicest of those souls.
>
> (ll. 1—16)

After showing the Roman poets Tibullus and Propertius marveling at the verses of the poet who almost excels them, Ronsard gives a farewell commendation to Marullus in the concluding stanzas:

> Dear soul, for the fair things
> Which I have found in thee
> Accept these pinks of little worth,
> These lilies fair, these fair roses.
>
> Ever may the earth rest light
> Upon thy bones, and on thy tomb
> Curling in many a branch
> Ever the green ivy twine.
>
> (ll. 36—44)

The pagan note of the epitaph, with its echo of Ovid's elegy for the death of Tibullus ("Et sic humus cineri non onerosa tuo. . ." from *Amores* III, ix) is the perfect choice for the imaginary tomb of Marullus, a strange neo-pagan. This tribute paid by Ronsard to one of his soulmates is a touching expression of admiration from the French poet to his master, the true link between himself and the ancient elegiac poets of Rome.

The light erotic verse of Marullus is freely adapted to various French stanza forms similar to those already used by Marot and his contemporaries. These charming poems break the monotony of the sonnets in the *Nouvelle Continuation des Amours* and give that collection its air of spontaneity, charm, and mannered grace, in some ways deceptively like the old-fashioned charm of Marot. And yet these songs are not really "marotique." Certainly they have many characteristics of Marot's light verse. But they do not have the attractive naïveté or the quaint turns of phrase. They are quite French and sometimes even popular in rhythm, sound, and words. But the same art hides the learning and skill that deceive the reader of the sonnets which are their companions. It is Ronsard the consummate craftsman who has learned his trade in the school of the ancients who has tuned these songs to accompany the fresh and elegantly costumed courtiers of the French Renaissance. He has learned from the ancients, from Marullus, from Marot and Saint-Gelais. But the song is his.

These songs have their own music in their words and rhythm, but they have been the most irresistible of all Ronsard's poems to composers who have set his words to music. And they were the favorites of courtiers and the wider public of his time. In the memoirs and chronicles of the Renaissance we can find accounts of their performance by choral groups (such as Baïf's academy of music or the musicians of the royal household) and of their being sung or hummed by lawyers, soldiers, and ladies accompanying themselves on the lute or guitar. One of these ladies was Mary Stuart, later Queen of Scots. The verbal music of these lyrics is, of course, untranslatable. The translations given here are meant only to convey the meaning of Ronsard's poems and to give some idea of their form.

One of the lyrics based on Marullus's epigrams is a little poem in the form of a dialogue between the poet and Cupid. It is by no means free of the mannerism of the Alexandrian poets whose imagery we have already encountered in the sonnets of *Amours I*. But it has a lightness of touch often missing in those poems. The text is that of the original version ("Amour, dy moy de grace. . ."):

Cupid, tell me I beg (so may the power
Of lowly mortals and of gods be ever in thy hands)
    Who gives thee arrows,
For always armed in a thousand places
Thou loosest thy shafts in the hearts of men and gods—
    Shafts armed with flame?

But tell me, I pray, is it not the god Mars
When he returns laden with the arms of men
    Slain in the battle?
Or else is it Vulcan who within his forges
(After thine are lost) makes for thee new ones
    And presents them to thee?

> Poor fool (Cupid answers) what? knowest thou not
> (Oh gentle slave of love!) the power and virtue
>   Of thy lady's fair eyes?
> The more arrows I shower upon men and gods,
> The more, in a moment, are given by the eyes
>   Of thy fair Marie.

It is difficult to imagine that this charming and mannered poem was transposed from Latin to French for a peasant lass. The preciousness of the conceits and the mythology (however obvious) do not have the popular tone which one associates with country wooing. Yet the song does have grace; and though it is not so direct and appealing as many of the *chansons* inspired by Marullus in the *Nouvelle Continuation* it does have delicacy and euphony, a subtle rhythm and form which create the musical mood. Part of Ronsard's success may be due to his use of the stanza form: two Alexandrine couplets followed by a half Alexandrine and rhyming *aabccb*. This stanza, so musical in the hands of a master poet, will be used by almost every generation of French poets till the end of the nineteenth century.

If Cupid as he appears in many of these *chansons* is the playful god of Alexandrian poetry, he can appear fearful, and his effects may be devastating in others. One of these songs on the state of physical torment is finely expressed in the *chanson* "Quand je te veux raconter mes douleurs. . .," a poem which I have vainly attempted to translate. A similar poem in which Ronsard conveys the almost trancelike state of desire and torment is inspired ultimately by a four-stanza fragment of Sappho, done in Latin by Catullus. Ronsard could have found the Greek text reprinted at the end of Estienne's *Anacreon.* Unlike Catullus, whose attitude toward the free adaptation of Greek models he usually shares, Ronsard has given a fairly close rendering of the Greek poem, though he uses two six-line stanzas of Alexandrine verse to render the four sapphic stanzas of the original. One important change has been made by Ronsard which affects the dramatic situation of the poem: Sappho's poem describes the passions aroused in her as she watches a young man and a girl together, whereas in Ronsard's version it is the poet himself who is with the girl. Here is a translation of the text of 1556, "Je suis un demidieu quand assis vis àvis . . .":

I am a demi-god when, seated face to face
With thee, my sweet care, I listen to thy words,
Words interrupted by a gracious smile,
A smile which holds my heart a captive,
For, looking at thine eyes, stricken, I faint,
And from my poor chest can draw no words.

My tongue grows thick, a subtle fire runs
Beneath my skin, I am deaf and dumb
And a dark night dwells upon my eyes
My blood is turned to ice, the spirit leaves my body,
I tremble from fear, and then almost it seems
That, lying at thy feet, languishing, I die.[4]

If we miss the intensity and directness of Sappho's masterpiece, the physical immediacy of her words, we do find much of the feeling of her poem here. (The more passionate physical aspects are in Ronsard's "Quand je te veux raconter mes douleurs. . .") One may object to the heart held prisoner (l.4) and to the rather weak rendering of the conclusion (ll. 11—12) where Ronsard omits the image of the pallor of the complexion like pale green grass, an image which he rightly knew would not pass into the language of his time. With these reservations we might say that Ronsard has written a musical and beautifully constructed poem.

The lyric qualities so evident in the shorter musical poems are not the least attractive feature of the longer *blasons* and elegies. In these more ample forms Ronsard often celebrates the world of nature and divine forces which animate it, or confides, as in a letter, his thoughts and personal life to a friend. Despite differences in form and compass, these poems are related to the more musical lyrics, for they contain passages similar in theme and treatment to their briefer companions in the same collections.

The same universe celebrated in the odes is present in these poems. It is an order rich in poetic subjects. To the hierarchical universe of the Middle Ages, in which each creature form smallest to greatest has a place and function, have been added the mythological universe of the ancients and the philosophical and natural speculations of the Renaissance. Ronsard lived and wrote before this magnificent synthesis was forever shattered by experimental sciences, mechanistic philosophies, and social upheavals. This universe, its every part alive and organic, gave the foundation and spirit to much of the finest nature poetry of the French Renaissance. Much of the richness of ornament, diversity of mood, and vitality of movement in Ronsard's poems on natural subjects may be attributed to his response to this world.

Ronsard and his friend Remy Belleau, both translators of Anacreon, blended in their poems on animals and flowers two traditions, the ancient and the medieval. The *blason* a medieval genre which sang the praise or blame of some object (animate or inanimate) or of some quality, had been revived in a famous contest sponsored by Clément Marot. Ronsard's first published poem, "Les Beautez qu'il voulait voir en s'amie" is in a certain sense a *blason* describing in detail the various anatomical charms of the poet's ideal lady. The *Elegie à Janet, peintre du Roy* (Laum. VI, 152ff.) is a more refined version of the early poem and shows Ronsard's continued interest in the descriptive poem.[5]

More interesting and more lyric are the *blasons* of the natural world. The first group is dedicated to Remy Belleau and in the *Bocage* of 1554 is followed by a poem of Belleau dedicated to Ronsard, "Le Papillon." Ronsard's poems praise the frog "La Grenouille" ("Nous t'estimons une Déessee. . ."), the wasp, "Le Freslon" ("Qui ne te chanteroi, Frelon?), and the ant, "La Fourmi" ("Puis que de moi tu as en don. . ."). Though the genre is medieval, and though Ronsard is perhaps more conservative in his development of the poem than Marot's disciples, the stamp of his classical learning is on every page. Each animal is provided with a myth, the frog and the wasp in particular receiving a veritable epyllion or miniature epic. Ronsard's meter, the old octosyllable of light French verse, gives his poems a lightness and movement difficult to achieve in a more ample line.

Similar to these *blasons* are poems dedicated to Jean Brinon, a *bon vivant* and patron of poets, to whom Ronsard dedicated his poem on mistletoe "Le Houx" ("Les uns chanteront le Fresne. . ."), twice the length of those dedicated to Belleau. To him Ronsard also dedicated three ambitious *blasons:* the *Elegie du Verre* ("Ceux que la Muse aimera plus que moi. . ."), an elaborate poem thanking Brinon for a gift of a goblet; *Les Armes* ("Quiconque a le premier des enfers déterrés. .") a veritable *contre-blason* denouncing the invention of arms, and especially of gunpowder; and finally *La Chasse* ("Te serai-je toujours redevable, Brinon?"), like the other poems inspired by a gift from Brinon and praising in this case the aristocratic pastime of which both Ronsard and his patrons were so fond. In each of these poems Ronsard has included passages of real lyric inspiration, though the form is the more ample Alexandrine couplet. For example in *La Chasse*, largely inspired by passages of the second book of Oppian's poem on hunting, the *Cynegetica*, Ronsard has interrupted his account of the activities of the hunt to paint an idyllic scene of rustic life (ll. 107–26). The rather pedestrian Greek of Oppian is transformed into the enticing country scene—grass, cool springs, cheese, milk, and wild strawberries, while shepherds drone a song into their bagpipes.

Also related to the *blason* in their praise of plants and animals are many odes of 1554–56. These odes or odelettes, though more lyric in form and tone, follow the pattern of the longer *blasons* in addressing the plant or animal, singing its praise, and bidding it farewell. Such are the ode to the hawthorn ("Bel Aubepin..."), to the swallow, "L'Arondelle" ("Si tost que tu sens arriver..."), to the nightingale ("Gentil Rossignol passager..."), and to the lark ("T'oseroit bien quelque poëte...").

Ronsard follows the Provençal and Italian poets in his preference for the nightingale and the lark, birds he often addresses in his poems. In the "Ode à l'Alouette" he blends two traditions, the medieval and the Anacreontic, and produces one of his most appealing *odes-blasons*. In the first stanza he announces his intention of praising the bird, finest of winged creatures and unequalled in its song. Then he shows a dawn scene with the peasant "wounding the earth with his plow" as the lark is already singing in the fields. The third stanza, a real masterpiece of music, describes in rhythm and sound the dawn song of the lark who, still covered with the dew of daybreak, makes a thousand speeches to the air, and "hanging in the sky" fills the air with song, "telling her loves to the winds." All this is rendered by the imitative sounds and repeating rhymes of Ronsard's stanza:

> Si tost que tu es arrosée,
> Au point de jour, de la rosée,
> Tu fais en l'air mille discours:
> En L'air des ailes tu fretilles
> Et pendue au ciel, tu babilles
> Et contes aux vents tes amours.[6]

Even poems which are, in content and form, the least lyric of the collections, show the musical gifts of Ronsard. One, *Le Narssis, pris d'Ovide* of the *Bocage* is addressed to a poet of the previous generation and, as its title indicates, is a retelling of the legend of Narcissus from Ovid's *Metamorphoses.* Although Ronsard will later retain it among his elegies in his collected editions, it is the prototype of the *Poeme,* a composition of moderate length on a variety of subjects.

Ronsard begins his poem by calling on his fellow poet to take down his musette, long unused through the winter, and to go out into the country, where already birds are singing, the melting snows are vanishing and the flowers, like the breasts of young girls, are showing their first buds. The ornaments of mythology, echoes of the odes of Horace, add color and life to the upward movement of the verse, with the French "Ja" *(déjà)* opening the lines as "iam" opens those of Horace. The spring scene now includes plants and animals taking their part in the universal renewal of nature, expressed in lyric movement and melody:

> Now against the sun the shrub of Bacchus
> Has donned its new gown, and the once widowed forest
> Bristles with new hair, and Ceres from heaven sees
> The wheat now forming a new crest for her crown,
> Now near the verdant bush, on the new grass,
> The gay shepherdesses twirl their distaffs,
> And with a long "Le-re-lot" to the neighboring forests
> And to the streams nearby confide their loves.

> (ll. 21-28)

Animals too join in the renewal of life moving in their appointed tasks and proclaiming the season of love:

> Now the turtle-doves in the wood recall their nest,
> Now pale and wan the doves cling beak to beak,
> Now the lark in the air fluttering its wings
> Warbles its loves, and the bee, feeding
> With its thighs on flowers, with its pleasant murmur
> Invites us to drowse upon the green sward
> Where Procne laments that the outraged honor
> Of Philomel her sister has not been avenged.

> (ll. 29-36)

In spite of the tag, "Taken from Ovid" in the title, many of the lyric and descriptive passages are not found in the *Metamorphoses* but in a number of sources, some perhaps still unidentified, some possibly forgotten by Ronsard himself, who had unconsciously absorbed them. Aside from the principal narrative, the poem is, in fact, a "contamination de textes." Not the least attractive among the parts of which it is composed (which actually blend much better into the composition than implied here) are those parts in which Ronsard combines his decorative description of flowers and birds with the evocative music of his poetry. Of all his successors only La Fontaine will recapture the magic dream of such lines as these on the bee:

> . . . . & l'avette, paissant
> De la cuisse les fleurs, de son plaisant murmure
> Invite à someiller sur la jeune verdure.

Another poem of the *Bocage, Epitre à Ambroise de La Porte, Parisien* is a very personal account of Ronsard's stay at his country living at Mareuil near Meaux where as the opening lines tell us he had taken refuge from the plague in Paris in the autumn of 1553. In spite of the "marotique" title *épitre*, usually avoided by Ronsard, and the informal opening, the poem combines description and narrative in a highly refined yet easy manner. As he so often does, Ronsard calls upon the figures of mythology to serve as ornaments and symbols, here of autumnal richness, wine and wheat. One should read the entire poem, but especially the passage in which Ronsard tells La Porte of his day in the country (ll. 17–66) with its descriptive and narrative elements so perfectly blended, its easy movement, and its unaffected references to characters from Vergil and Homer, whose works Ronsard sings to his guitar. The reverie is interrupted by a veritable Bacchic procession, the peasants of Champagne harvesting the grapes and preparing the vintage.

Here is the opening of Ronsard's account of a day in the country; even without the sound of the French one can perhaps appreciate the easy movement from one style to another and the lyric quality which lifts the account from mere verse narrative to the level of poetry:

> From morning when saffron-colored Dawn
> Has brought back the brightness of fair day
> And from noon till the setting rays,
> Aimless I wander lost in the fields
> Sniffing the air, gazing at lovely meadows

> Contemplating the hills covered with vines
> Looking from afar at the heavy apple trees
> Almost broken by their Autumnal fruit,
> On the delicate green grass tapping
> The little ball with my racquet's strokes,
> Watching the boats float by on the Marne,
> Hiding myself among the reeds of islets. . .
>
> (ll. 17-28)

From the "poetic" paraphrase of the opening line, Homeric in tone, with its saffron-colored dawn, we move easily to the poet himself, who then casually as it were describes his pastimes, though in reality never completely abandoning the descriptive and lyric movement for the trite and personal, yet never pompous and frigidly neoclassical. This delicate balance, perhaps more common in English poetry, is rare in French; this delicate balance of the intimate and yet universal, the picturesque and the natural, lyric and narrative, is one of Ronsard's magic touches possessed by few poets in France.

CHAPTER 6

The Hymnes

I *A New Genre of Poetry*

COMPOSED and published at the same time as the *Continuations* were Ronsard's two books of *Hymnes*—Book I (1555) and Book II (1556)—nearly parallel in date the lighter verse of the *Continuations.* Just as the *Continuations* are, in a sense, a development of one aspect of the lighter poetry of the *Odes,* the hymns are related to the more serious odes, whether Pindaric or other. The hymns are related as well in source and theme to some of the "nature poems" of earlier collections and in particular to the *blasons* of the *Bocage* and *Meslanges* with their descriptions of plants and animals mingled with philosophical and moral comments.

The poems of the two books are not the first of Ronsard's work to bear the title "hymn." Earlier he had published his *Hymne de la France,* a hymn for St. Gervaise (patron of his parish church), a hymn to night, and, for the memorial volume dedicated to the sister of François I, the *Hymne triumphal sur le trepas de Marguerite de Valois,* a work appropriately Christian and Medieval in its battle between the flesh and the spirit. Ronsard's reworking of a *Hymne de Bacchus* in Alexandrine couplets (1553) points toward the form which dominates in the present collections: rhymed couplets in twelve-syllable lines, henceforth called by him "vers heroiques." Since the hymns, unlike the odes, were not composed for a musical setting, Ronsard could use this form already found in the sonnets and elegies of the *Continuations;* in his mind this verse must have corresponded to the hexameter of his classical models. The publication of the four collections of 1555-56 revealed for the first time the rich possibilities of this poetic line, destined to become in his hands, and in those of his successors, the French verse par excellence.[1]

The apologies for the exquisite short poems already studied in connection with the *Continuations* might indicate that Ronsard had renounced his ambition to compose a French national epic. This "long poëme," which would require a supreme effort, had long been announced by the poets of the new school; its plot had often been given in poems written for the king, who had "commanded" Ronsard to begin the work. But the ecclesiastical preferments which would provide the leisure for such a task were not forthcoming; Ronsard's lyre was not "croziered" with a rich endowment from an abbey. Yet he had not given up all hope. Instead, he turned to patrons who might be helpful. If Henri II was not yet an Augustus, there might still be a Maecenas at court. Hence the number of poems, beginning with the *Odes* and continuing into the 1560's, dedicated or addressed to powerful courtiers who, as well as patronizing artists and poets, had the king's ear when favors were granted.

The most notable among these powerful magnates to whom Ronsard appealed in the hymns was the family of Coligny-Chastillon, whose members are lauded in particular in Book I. The dedication of the book is addressed to Odet de Coligny, Cardinal de Chastillon, called throughout the poems "mon Maecene." Other members of this ancient family were Anne de Montmorency, Constable of France, uncle of the cardinal; the cardinal's younger brothers, Gaspard de Coligny, Grand Admiral of France; and François D'Andelot, Colonel-General of the Infantry. All are included in an allegorical poem in a peculiar style, the poetic "temple" erected to their glory by the poet *(Le Temple de Messeigneurs Le Connetable et des Chastillons)*, dedicated to the cardinal. In addition Ronsard dedicated to him the *Hymne de la Philosophie* and the *Hercule Chrestien* in the same book. In the second book the *Hymne de Pollux et de Castor*, one of his most elaborate compositions, is addressed to Gaspard de Coligny. Ronsard was obviously depending on the support of this influential family, and in particular of the cardinal, for making his way at court. His hopes were disappointed when the brothers, after 1560, openly espoused the cause of the French Protestants.[2]

The arch rival of this family was the House of Guise, the dukes and princes of Lorraine. Henri, Duc de Guise, was the greatest military hero of the reign. His brother Charles, Cardinal de Lorraine, was the most powerful minister in the king's council. Both were uncles of Mary

Stuart, heiress to the crown of Scotland and destined to become the queen of the dauphin François. Though more powerful than Chastillon, the Cardinal de Lorraine was less warmly addressed by Ronsard. Eventually he proved to be indifferent to the poet, who expressed his bitter disappointment in a witty and trenchant allegorical poem, *Le Proces* (written in 1561; published in 1565). In the imaginary lawsuit which gives the work its title, the haughty prelate is tried and found wanting in promises of patronage. This is the last work of importance addressed to him.

Both these families are glorified in the opening *Hymne du Treschrestien Roy de France Henry II, de ce nom,* a long (776 lines) and somewhat disorganized work flattering in the loftiest style the virtues and accomplishments of the king. As in the *Odes* addressed to the monarch Ronsard calls on his great store of erudition and his recent readings in epic literature to decorate the work with myths and fables: the battle of the Gods and the Titans, Castor and Pollux, and briefer metaphors and comparisons are all meant to give evidence of Ronsard's ability to undertake the composition of a great epic. Here again the king appears as Jupiter; his marital qualities are particularly stressed. Since the poem is an open appeal for favor, Ronsard also lays emphasis on the king's liberality. (Richness and largesse are important themes of the hymns; needless to say the poet hoped to receive his share of them.)[3] Here is a passage which is typical of many:

> As for that virtue which lifts thee nearest Heaven,
> It is Liberality; after the example of the Gods,
> Who bestow in abundance, esteeming Avarice
> (As truly it is) the school of all vice. . . .

Later in the same poem he continues:

> No Artisan is seen, excelling in his Art,
> No Mason, Painter, Poet, nor daughty Swordsman
> To whom thy open hand does not freely grant
> Some present worthy of his fair artifice.
> And this is the reason, O magnanimous King,
> That each one seeks thee out, desiring to sing of thee.

Perhaps Ronsard knew that this was more fancy than fact, for he also praised the king's father, François I, famous for his patronage of letters.

As though seeking to include Henri II in this liberality Ronsard introduces a mythological scene at the cradle of Henri in which celestial and terrestrial divinities in French guise predict a glorious reign. This passage leads to a lengthy "louange de France," a device which allows the poet to include the entire kingdom in his praise. For Ronsard, as for many writers previous to 1789, the king was the personification of the kingdom. The praise of royalty, which so often rings like a forced note in modern republican ears, was in fact the most usual way for poets to express patriotism. Here Ronsard can draw on Pindaric and Alexandrian poets, as well as on Vergil and Horace. In surveying the richness of France, her fertile lands, her variety of climates, her forests, mines, and rivers, Ronsard praises her citizens in the traditional division by estates. Peasants, artisans, scholars, and knights appear, followed by the great military heroes and by the king himself. But who will recall the glories of this reign without the poet's record?

> A King, howsoever great in land or prowess
> Dies like a farmhand, inglorious, unless he leave
> Some record of himself, and this record comes not
> After death, unless the Muse be willing
> To grant it to him who gently invites her
> And with a decent favor recompenses her merit.
> Others, too, have this power: Bellay, a Jodelle,
> A Baïf, Pelletier, a Belleau, and Tiard
> Who from the nine Sisters received the fair art
> Of granting through verse new life to great Lords,
> Far better than buildings or casts of bronze.

And so the hymn, repetitious, exaggerated, and prolix as it is at times (it was greatly reduced in later editions) draws to its conclusion with a favorite theme: *la gloire.* To it is joined the praise of liberality and the contrast of the lasting glory bestowed by true poetry, the gift of the Muses, with the transitory nature of material monuments. An ancient commonplace, to be sure, but one nonetheless warmly felt and frequently voiced by Ronsard, who here associates his fellow poets in one of the lists which gave rise to the myth of the "Pléiade." But Henri II was deaf to Ronsard's pleas; his liberality went to sculptors and architects, and the Muse continued to beg in vain.

Though perhaps the least attractive aspect of the *Hymnes,* this element of praise is an important part of the collection, and one which is frequently overlooked. The poet is obviously using the new poems to seek support for his ambitions and to reconcile former enemies. Each book and each poem contains opening passages addressed to the powerful or influential. In addition to these epistles, elegies and epitaphs are included, all directed to the same purpose.[4] Thus, in a sense, the collection has certain features in common with the epistles of Horace, who, like Ronsard, had abandoned for a while the intricate lyric form of his odes for the middle style of the verse-letter. Unlike Horace, whose independence and position were securely established at the time of his epistles, the Renaissance poet was still forced to seek the patronage which would secure his career. Thus the praise of the king and of the great families of his court, which may seem to us base flattery, was imposed upon Ronsard by the circumstances of his precarious position.

One should not assume, however, that Ronsard was always hypocritical in his lavish use of incense or in his likening of the great to the gods of Olympus. This same procedure, already found in the *Odes* (where the Valois court becomes a veritable pantheon) has ample precedent in antiquity. The comparison of the great to gods, demigods, and heroes of myth and legend was a well-established Renaissance custom, one which was to reach its apogee in France during the reign of Louis XIV, for whom poets and artists devised elaborate mythological schemes strikingly similar to those of the Valois court. For some of the lords and ladies thus praised Ronsard had true admiration. There can be no doubt that he felt the esteem and gratitude so often expressed by all the poets of the Pléiade for Marguerite de France. Her learning and courage did deserve the title of Pallas-Minerva. As for her brother Henri II, Ronsard, in spite of disappointments, could still speak truly of his knightly virtues. For the Duc de Guise, the poet had similar feelings of respect, though for his brother the Cardinal de Lorraine one notes a certain reserve and, later, real disaffection. Anne de Montmorency, uncle of the Coligny brothers, was by no means faultless as a diplomat or a military strategist; yet Ronsard passes these weaknesses by and sees him as the embodiment of the great feudal qualities so admired by his class: bravery, loyalty to Altar and Throne.[5] For him Ronsard composed one of his finest and most elaborate epitaphs; its magnificent closing lines evoke the old warrior's victories and portray for his descendants the ideal funeral cortege:

> In place of marble and rich colored pillars,
> Inter the Dead in these poetic lines
> And do him honor with our Poetry.
> A Column, in the end, falls to mould
> And sepulchres by age are overcome,
> But not the verses sung by the Muse.
> Banish from this those funeral rites,
> Those black garments, those torches in shadows,
> Tears and groans. Let his corselet march,
> Pierced and bloody; let his gauntlet march,
> His helmet, his lance, and his standard.
> Let the drum, the fife, and the trumpet,
> Thundering to Heaven in roaring chords
> With virile sound march before his corpse,
> And let such sound crush Death herself.

For the supreme virtues of the nobility Ronsard could forget whatever failings the old Constable had shown, and praise him, "As one who died in unvanquished Faith To uphold his Church and his King."

No such loyalty for "Church and King" could be claimed by the Coligny family after 1560. The cardinal, the admiral, and their younger brother all embraced the Protestant faith and, in the case of Gaspard and D'Andelot, took up arms to fight for their convictions. Ronsard, who became a leading voice in the expression of Catholic loyalty in the same decade, can be excused for deleting several dedications and poems addressed to this family from later collected editions. His true feelings for Odet de Coligny, however, should be judged not from these deletions but from the dedications and passages which he retained through every subsequent edition, including the posthumous text of 1587. They, and not the omissions so easily explainable by circumstances, show the poet's esteem and devotion to one who had been his Maecenas and from whom religious differences, exile, and death eventually separated him.[6]

Important as is the place of praise and of the epistolary character of the opening passages of the hymns, it is not these features which occasionally lift these poems to the level of greatness. Perhaps it was these very features, together with a certain looseness of composition and prolixity of expression which led Sainte-Beuve to call them "unreadable." Ronsard, often severer on his own poems than any other critic, later pruned from the hymns dozens of passages, some exceeding a hundred lines. The poems as they appear in 1578 are already considerably reduced; by 1584 many more passages are gone. Most of these omissions seem justified; only in a few instances do we feel that the poem has lost.[7] Rather it seems to have gained in unity of structure and tone. Often the passage is a personal digression addressed to the patron, or else repetition.

II   *The Orphic Voice*

As the name of the genre suggests there is a sacred connotation which is inseparable from the word "hymn." In its earliest form it may have evoked the magical power of a divinity; later the divinity or demigod is praised either by naming his attributes or temples, or by an additional narrative passage in mythical, allegorical, or lyric mode celebrating conquests or triumphs. The hymn is then in a sense an offering of praise and celebration as well as a prayer for aid. It is the combination of all these elements together with the epistle offering the hymn as a gift that gives the Ronsardian poems their peculiar originality. Praised by his contemporaries, especially the learned, scorned by certain critics puzzled by their apparently unresolved clashes of tone and theme, the hymns offer a rich treasure of some of Ronsard's most splendid and majestic verse.[8]

If Ronsard's praise is often bestowed upon the person to whom he presents the hymn and upon the subject which he treats, his loftiest praise is reserved for the central myth or allegory. This, in turn, magnifies the value of his gift and its glory or solemnity is reflected upon the receiver. Thus, in the *Hymne de la Philosophie,* Odet de Coligny receives added luster from the celebration of wisdom and knowledge leading to virtue, which is the core of the poem. Similarly the Cardinal de Lorraine's role as diplomat and minister of the royal council is closely related to the myth of Justice in the hymn to that divinity. As has been shown by several critics, the recipient of the poem is closely bound, in Ronsard's mind, and in the poem itself, with the theme and with the devices through which it is developed: myth, allegory, and descriptive passages.[9]

Not only are there subtle correspondences between recipient, theme, myth, and allegory, but there are equally subtle ties binding one hymn to another. The Coligny family appears in the dedication to Book I. in the *Hymne de Henri II,* the *Temple des Chastillon,* the *Hymne de la Philosophie,* and the *Hercule Chrestien.* Their personal qualities are always linked with the virtues celebrated in the hymn. The same family appears in Book II in the dedication of the elaborate miniature myth *L'Hymne de Pollox et de Castor,* appropriately offered to Gaspard de Coligny, Admiral of France, so closely linked with his brother D'Andelot; both are reflected in the exploits of the mythical demigods of the poem.

The three hymns of Book II (ed. of 1556) are joined even more closely in dedication and even by text. The entire book is a present to Marguerite de France, already praised in the opening poem of Book I. To her are presented the *Hymne de l'Eternité* and the hymn which follows, a miniature epic, *L'Hymne de Calais et de Zetes.* At the end of this second hymn, celebrating the victories of those flighty but pugnacious twins of the Argo, Ronsard introduces the final hymn, which also celebrates fraternal demigods. He takes leave of his heroes:

> Your hymn is finished, I shall praise you no more
> I now wish to recall Castor and Pollox,
> Children of Zeus: I wish to make their renown,
> As I have made yours, forever famous.
>
> *Hymne de Calais et de Zetes,*
> (11. 719–22)

Themes and images too numerous to mention also bind the hymns together. The triumphant and heroic notes which open the *Hymne de Henri II* (the first poem of Book I) are the overture to the presentation of the final hymn of Book II. Other triumphs are celebrated: of Learning over Ignorance (in passages to Marguerite de France and in the *Hymne de la Philosophie*); the triumph of virtue in the same hymn has echoes in the hymn on justice and in other passages, such as the tributes to the Grand Constable; the triumph of faith over death, as in the *Hymne de la Mort* and the *Hercule Chrestien* and the *Hymne de l'Eternité.*

Perhaps the most striking unity of the hymns is found in the cosmic setting, the scene of triumphs and defeats, the actions of men and beasts, birds, spirits, and deities. Ronsard's cosmos is still the hierarchical universe of the Middle Ages made more awesome by the occult and scientific interests of his age. It is a universe in which the sublunar world is a place of change and flux, while beyond, in the realm of planets and fixed stars, the divinities which serve God are changeless and eternal. It is a universe in which fate and destiny, aided by lesser creatures and obeying the laws of God, rule the actions of all creatures. It is a universe alive with omens, influences, spirits, with signs and wonders filling the poet with delight, awe, and a gnawing apprehension. In this world—part Greek, part medieval, and barely modern—the deeds of men and gods are expressed in terms of nature and myth, allegory and symbol, but all in a strangely concrete fashion. Far more than the mechanical universe of Descartes and Newton it is a world made for poetry.

Even critics who fail to appreciate the hymns as a genre agree that the collection contains passages of unsurpassed grandeur. They have had no difficulty in making an anthology of lines from the hymns illustrating Ronsard's claims as a philosophic (in the sixteenth-century sense) poet, or as an orphic bard. At times he does achieve those orphic qualities which he prays for in the opening of the *Hymne de l'Eternité:*

> Filled with a fire divine kindled in my soul
> Following in Orpheus' feet I would more loftily
> Disclose the secrets of Nature and of the Skies,
> Sought out by a mind unused to sloth.
> I would, were I but able, receive at last the praise
> Of her who never through the years is changed,
> But rather herself changes the ages and the times,
> The months, the seasons, and inconstant days,
> Herself changeless, for she is not subjected,
> Being Queen and mistress, to the laws she has made.

(ll. 1-10)

Such is the ambition and the goal of Ronsard. For such an undertaking he seeks the favor of divine inspiration so that his poetry, like Eternity whom he sings, will outlast time:

> Of thy favor grant me, O vast Eternity,
> The power to tell of thy great deity,
> Grant me a bow of brass, an iron lyre,

> Grant strings of steel, a tempered voice,
> That so my song may last so long
> As thou in Heaven perpetually dwell.
> Thou Queen of years, of ages and of worlds,
> Who hold as thy heritage all the Heavens,
> The first among the Gods, far from the cares
> And mortal toil which torment us below,
> In thyself content, and blessed in thyself,
> Dwelling in plenitude without travail.
>
> *(Hymne de l'Eternité,* ll. 15-26)

The cares and toils of mortals are not absent from this cosmic verse. They form, in fact, the central portion of the *Hymne des Astres,* dedicated to Ronsard's former enemy, Mellin de Saint-Gelais. After a propitiatory opening, Ronsard describes in the hymn proper the early existence of the Stars, who like a flock are shepherded through the fields of heaven by the Hours. They are unconcerned with men or animals. Then follows the myth of the assault of the Titans on Olympus, and the role of the Stars in bringing them to defeat. As the Giants scale the mountain, the Stars flash their brilliant light and blind the rebels. Jupiter then fixes them in the heavens and gives them control over the destinies of the creatures of earth.

> Since then, all birds which fly or sing,
> All silent fish, which haunt the waves,
> And all beasts of the field or of the wood
> Or cavernous mounts, were enslaved to their laws.
> But above all man, whose life is held a subject
> To the destiny composed by Heaven through Stars,
> Man, who first dared to understand their ways
> And gave them in the Sky the names he pleased.
>
> *(Hymne des Astres,* ll. 101-108)

All the estates of men, high and low, are then described in a series of remarkable tableaux; this subject, a frequent one in Ronsard's work, displays his understanding of all the conditions of the men of his time, from great rulers to the humble plowmen and vintners whom he had known since childhood. All are under the mysterious influence of the stars. Finally, the stars are messengers and prophets of seasons, and most important, of future calamities. "For [they] are the sacred writings of God,/ Or rather yet great God's faithful secretaries" (ll. 205-6), and like good secretaries they keep their secret. Even the lines on the hands and faces of men, which might reveal the future, are mysteries:

> But from want of understanding these lines
> Which are our very own, we fail to comprehend
> What God writes for us, and never foreseeing
> The evil to come, we always fall again,
> After one misfortune, into yet another one.

(ll. 217-21)

These cares and anxieties do not affect the Stars, who are beyond the realm of change and flux:

> Such care concerns you not, for after our birth
> When you have filled us with your gifts
> You pay no heed to us, nor to our deeds:
> But move on in your course, loosed from care,
> Free from the passions which follow from their cradle
> Men who here below live bowed down with woe.

(ll. 245-50)

The hymn ends with a typical closing address to the divinity, a praise of the divine Stars:

> I greet you, Children of the first night,
> Blessed Stars divine, through whom all are moved.
> While you turn ever in your ordered dance
> In Heaven, I shall fulfill below the fate
> Which you pleased to give me, good or bad, when
> Into my frame entered my eternal soul.

(ll. 252-56)

Within the limits of this study it is hardly possible to do justice to this rich collection. One can only point to the variety of tone and subject—the solemnity of the *Hymne de la Mort,* perhaps the finest of all the hymns; the conversational arguments and ironic asides of the *Hymne de l'Or*: the whimsical and humorous and frightening demonic lore of the *Hymne des Daemons*; the brilliant narrative and descriptive passages in the miniature epics of Book II. At their best the hymns show, as well as any major poems, Ronsard's breadth of culture and sensitivity, his supreme command of rhythms, of periodic structure, of sounds and roots of words, his mastery of the great Alexandrine couplet, and his successful integration of the world of Greek fable and lore into his own speech and time for the full harmonization of the great themes of philosophical and speculative poetry.

III   *The Hymns of the Four Seasons*

In his first book of the *Recueil des Nouvelles Poësies* (1563-64) Ronsard published four new hymns celebrating the seasons of the year. According to Laumonier, the first in order of composition appears to have been summer (*l'Hymne de l'Esté*) followed by spring, autumn, and winter.

Like the hymns of 1555-56, these are dedicated to friends or patrons, and each opens with a fairly extensive address to the recipient. Three of these (*L'Esté, L'Autumne,* and *L'Hiver*) are really statements of Ronsard's poetic credo, beginning with his contributions to the hymn as a genre, then recounting a famous poetic autobiography and rephrasing his beliefs concerning the mission of the poet, and finally his reiteration of the supremacy of inspiration and the supreme merits of the true poet.

Ronsard's claims to originality in these hymns seem to be well founded if one does not interpret the word in a modern sense. Few poets of the Renaissance would write an ambitious work such as these hymns without drawing on models, and Ronsard is no exception. But by combining his sources and adding his own poetic skills, he has indeed produced something new. Thus the "burlesque" poems of Folengo may have provided the original impetus for these "new" hymns, but the elaboration of these humorous poems into a superior work of art is Ronsard's alone. As usual he draws on all his vast reading, his sense of the concrete image, of colorful and elaborate detail, and his feeling for myth, symbol, and allegory animated by narrative, humor, and his musical verse to produce something uniquely his own.

Each of the four hymns has a similar structure: an introductory statement of theme, followed by an address on some aspect of Ronsard's conception and practice of poetry; then comes the hymn proper, with the mythical account of the loves of gods and divine forces personified, stories of their offspring and their exploits; and a final salutation to the season, concluding with a brief prayer for favor toward the recipient of the poem.

Certain themes also recur in the hymns. That of fecundity in the world of nature, already seen in the odes, seems to be dominant. It is a theme as ancient as literature, to which the ancient poets devoted some of their finest verses. It is also a theme dear to Ronsard, one of which he began at this time of his life to realize the supreme importance. Others are the function and work of the elements, the variety and richness of nature, and the humor which results from incongruity.

The earliest hymn, possibly, and certainly the one closest in concept to the "burlesque" poems of Folengo, shows Ronsard's rich talent mastering the disparate sources of his poem, the *Hymne de l'Esté.* Though not so well known as the hymn to autumn,[10] with its famous lines on the poet as prophet and divine interpreter, this summer hymn is typical of the collection. After announcing his intention to praise this season, Ronsard tells Robertet de Fresne that he is presenting a new kind of poem. We have already seen what may have been meant by this claim, a claim presented in the imagery of Horace and Propertius. Then we enter the hymn proper, if not directly the subject announced in the title. Nature, a young wife married to an old and impotent husband, Time, complains in explicit terms of her dissatisfaction. The mismatch, the subject of comic laughter for hundreds of years, is forcefully presented, and with considerable humor. Nature, having unsuccessfully sought to arouse the passion of her decrepit spouse, announces that marital fidelity is for mere mortals but not binding on the gods, who are free and live in another realm. She then seeks the youthful and vigorous Sun, to whom she declares in splendid forthright fashion her desire and its purpose, fertility of the earth. From their union are born the four seasons. As a gift to her new friend, Nature presents the Sun with a gorgeous golden chariot fashioned by Vulcan (and described by Ronsard with all the lavish detail one would expect of a lover of the arts). Then Nature procedes to go and placate and deceive her doddering husband.

The poem is well over half finished when the subject, Summer, is quickly introduced. As is the way with gods, he rapidly grows to manhood and soon consummates his union with Ceres, thereby bringing the imperfect flowers of Spring to fruition:

> Of what use are flowers if the fruit does not ripen?
> Of what use is the wheat, if the spikes are not golden?
> All things have their end, and move toward a goal,
> Destiny has willed it, such is the covenant
> Of Nature and of God, by ordering of Fate.

> (ll. 197-202)

Then, as the hymn draws to a close, Ronsard, like so many poets of the Renaissance, in a veritable litany, celebrates the Summer and his emblem the Sun:

> I greet thee, O Summer, prince of the year,
> Child of the Sun, who has endowed thee with strength,
> Father, provider, nurturer, wheat- and corn-giver,
> Viril, perfect, whole, all powerful, divine,
> Resplendent with rays, thou guidest from afar
> The Sun who in the morning bridles his steeds,
> Longed for by mortals, crowned with sheaves,
> Symbol and figure of the full years of man,
> Who forgest the lightning and the thunderbolts,
> Sailor, traveller, courier, man of war.

> (ll. 217-26)

We may not agree with Ronsard's contemporary and admirer, Estienne Pasquier, who found these four hymns the most perfect of Ronsard's poetry, but we should be doing him and ourselves an injustice if we dismiss them as stale allegory and artificial verse-making. Like many of his longer poems, they all include lines, and entire passages, of the highest order, of the kind of poetry that could be written only during the Renaissance, and only by Ronsard.

CHAPTER 7

Ronsard, Poète Engagé: Political and Religious Poems (1559-1563)

1 The End of a Decade (1550-1560)

THE solicitation of patronage and the receiving of favors, however disappointing they might be, had marked Ronsard as a court poet. With patronage came burdens which could not be shrugged off lightly: attendance at court and the composition of all kinds of verse. These verses might celebrate great events or trifling episodes; they might commemorate a royal birth, or marriage; express in conventional formulas the amorous dalliance of some great lord; provide lyrics for royal entertainments, the epitaph of a favorite lap dog or a great military leader. To all these tasks Ronsard brought his great talent and his fifteen years of experience as a poet, so that among the most banal and hackneyed of forms and themes we find traces of that genius which marks his work as superior to all others of its kind.

Another aspect of Ronsard's position at court becomes apparent from 1559 onwards: his role as adviser and counsellor to the crown and, in a wider sense, the voice of royal policy and spokesman for a great number of his fellow citizens. The *Poëte du Roy* (as he was called by the officials of the Jeux Floraux in Toulouse in 1554) is one and the same as the *poète engagé*. As is so often true in his life, Ronsard finds himself at once the courtier catering to the whims of the great and the critic of the court and its corruption, the panegyrist of the crown and its severest critic.[1] The scores of poems which Ronsard wrote in this apparently dual capacity range from the numerous verses written halfheartedly at the behest of patrons to the magnificent poems composed during the outbreak of the civil-religious wars.

The years 1559 and 1560 must have seemed to Ronsard like the summation of a decade of feverish poetic activity and the beginning of a new and far-from-glorious career as a pensioned versifier. The death of his former rival Mellin de Saint-Gelais (1559), Ronsard's appointment as *conseiller* and *aumosnier ordinnaire du Roy,* and the publication in 1560 of his first collected edition, all mark a stage in his career and seem to point toward the fulfillment of his ambitions to be the royal poet par excellence. But the *Second Livre des Meslanges* (1559), like many collections both before and after that date, is filled with dedications to influential officials and powerful courtiers, pleas for patronage, increasingly bitter statements of disappointments, and longing for freedom from the servitude of the court. Conscious of his superiority, Ronsard was also well aware of his dependence on favors too often granted to less deserving rivals. In the autobiographical epistles (often called *élégies*) found in the *Meslanges* and *Poëmes* of 1559-60 these are recurring themes. Two poems addressed to his Maecenas, Cardinal Odet de Coligny, are typical: The *Elegie,* opening the *Meslanges,* and the *Complainte contre Fortune.* In spite of the favors of the cardinal, Fortune (a figure who appears frequently in Ronsard's verse) has played the poet false. She is "hostile, inconstant, flighty/Deaf, dumb, blind, ungrateful and untruthful/ Evil, deceitful, abominable and foul,/ And worthy (as she is) of wearing woman's dress" (Laum,X,17). Before he had known the cardinal's favor, the poet had been happy and free of ambition. He paints a scene of his youthful inspiration, a theme which is beautifully developed in three important poems of the period. Here is the earliest, from the *Complainte . . .*:

> Before I was your man, I lived in calm;
> Now upon the streams, now in a retreat,
> Within a hidden grove, now through meadows
> I wandered, the nursling of the holy Muses nine.
> No rock there was which I could not unlock,
> No cave went undiscovered by my eye,
> No fair spring of water was untouched by my hand,
> No vale so deep in which I entered not.
> Golden-locked Phoebus presented me his lute,
> Pan the woodland god gambolled to my flutes
> And together with Sylvans the gentle Dryads
> Trod the green in sprightly dances to my songs.
>   (ll. 79-90)

Then Ronsard tells of his great efforts to create a new poetry in France, another theme often treated in subsequent poems, and most beautifully and succinctly expressed in his epitaph. In this version we are reminded of the struggles with critics and rivals:

> ... With great effort I was the very first
> Who led the Muses from Greece into France,
> The first who measured their steps to my cadence
> And in place of the speech of Greece and Rome,
> The first who had them speak the tongue of France.
> Boldly I set myself against the ignorant mob,
> And the louder it cried, the fiercer it became
> To rend my name, the more it slandered me,
> The more courageous I; my strength took fire
> Against this crowd, and imitating a thousand things
> Divinely hidden in the books of Greece,
> I made new words, I restored the old,
> Giving slight heed to the common horde, envious,
> Backbiting and ignorant, who since have praised
> My verse, which first they held in scorn.
>
> (ll. 96-110)

Then, says Ronsard, "I learned the way to the Louvre" and learned the way to bend my proud nature to the ways of the court. And so the Muses, neglected by him, have fled, leaving him the victim of delusions of future grandeur and the plaything of Fortune.

If Ronsard felt that his career at court was in a sense the betrayal of the Muses, he felt as well that the fruitful years of intense youthful poetic inspiration had passed away, leaving him old and dull at thirty-five. He expresses these sentiments in a passage remarkable for its vivid simile—a passage greatly admired later by Sainte-Beuve and Victor Hugo:

> As in September in Angevine casks one sees
> The youth of wines bubbling and foaming,
> Which in its cradle rumbles with great sound
> And would of a sudden escape from out its bonds,
> Ardent, impatient, and ever restless
> To swell, to foam, to burst forth in great jets,
> Until the cold of winter has overcome its strength
> Locking up its power in the prisoning bark,

> Thus does poetry in the season of youth
> Boil up in our hearts, scarce retained by sense,
> The slave of appetite, which loftily stirs up
> The magnanimous fury of a lusty poet.
>
> (*Elegie au seigneur L'Huilier,*
> (ll. 23-34)

The "poëte gaillard" follows the great, seeks favors; he is restless, full of passions, haughty, disdainful, caring only for himself, believing he is a god. This seems quite likely a portait of the author at the time when he was composing his odes and first *Amours*.

Now, at thirty-five, his blood cools, his brow is furrowed with wrinkles. Then the Muse flees, the spring of Pegasus is dried up, the laurels wither. Again we seem to have a kind of self-portrait, merciless as are many of those Ronsard composed in his later years. We sense the presence of commonplaces used in the ancient poets, but the feeling that this is Ronsard as he sees himself in 1560 persists. Now his youthful inspiration is gone; now it is too late to compose the great work for which he has sought in vain over a decade the encouragement and support of the court. "It angers me to see, now that I am old,/ A dull protonotary, a spiteful foppish youth" receive undeserved favors. Rich prebends and abbeys are given to "an old trowel" (Ronsard's enemy, the architect Philibert de L'Orme) or to foreigners, mostly Italians. The poem ends on a note of bitter discouragement: Ronsard, who has tried all means for continuing his work, is so discouraged that he must beg for help and sends this "unpleasant letter" to be forwarded to a royal treasurer.

Just at this juncture in his career Ronsard was led out of his impasse by force of circumstances. The events of 1560-63 turned him suddenly into a path which he had seemed only gazing towards. The accidental death of Henri II, the brief and unhappy reign of his eldest son François II, the coronation of Charles IX, and the outbursts of violence which led to the first of the civil, dynastic, religious wars—all these events forced Ronsard to enter the lists as a champion of King and Church. Thus his position at court, which had seemed to limit him to the most superficial themes and banal occasional verse, had placed him at this critical moment in the thick of intrigue and action. Pierre de Ronsard, court poet and pensioner, became a *poète engagé*.

II *Patriotic Poetry (1559-1560)*

Even before the beginings of the civil-religious crisis of 1560-63
Ronsard had begun to take his role as *Poëte du Roy* quite seriously.
The *Exhortation* to the royal troups (1559) fighting in the Flanders
campaign rings with thrilling passages of an unmistakable patriotic tone.
Ronsard always excelled in capturing the movement and sound of
battle in his verse; one detects not only the admirer of the ancients who
sang of battle, but even more the companion-at-arms of Henri II and
the pupil of the Royal Riding Academy. But his concern is not to
glorify war and conquest, but rather to urge his countrymen to defend
their homeland:

> Noble sons of Mars, your combat is not
> For a tourney's prize, for a base reward;
> You combat for yourselves, for your family,
> To keep secure your homes, your aging fathers,
> Who, praying God for you, stretch their hands to Heaven.
>
> *(Exhortation au Camp du Roy . . .*
> (ll. 88-92)

Even more patriotic in tone, and perhaps more in keeping with
Ronsard's own feeling, is the following *Exhortation pour la Paix*,
composed on the occasion of the peace of Cateau-Cambrésis marking
the end of the dynastic wars with the Empire and the French
excursions into Italy. Here ancient and biblical passages recall the
horrors and devestation of war contrasted with the blessing of peace.[2]
Already in his "contre-blason" *Les Armes* (1554) Ronsard had depicted
the ravages and slaughter introduced by firearms and armaments, the
diabolical invention of gunpowder and its attendant destruction. Here
he urges the French to obey the pacific creed of Christ (ll. 1-26). If
they must fight, let them return to the Holy Land to deliver the sacred
cities from the hand of the Infidel. What good will come from fighting
in Europe, he asks:

> Even when you have fought, and split your heads
> For twenty or thirty years, still the conquest
> Of our Kings will not exceed a handsbreadth,
> And a hundred thousand men will die in vain

> Around a frozen village, or some poor town,
> Or a small castle, to bring it to surrender.

(ll. 51-56)

Once, says Ronsard, recalling the myth of the Golden Age and the reign of Saturn, men lived in peace and contentment. It is for this time that the poet longs:

> Alas! Why did I not live in that happy time
> Instead of the time when nimble Faith flew off
> From the vicious world, leaving in her place
> Only war and death, fraud and deceit.
> Alas! Then I should not see so many corpses,
> So many heaps of dead who fertilize the fields,
> So many horses slain, now free of their burdens,
> Stopping the course of the Moselle or the Somme,
> Squeeze in ruddy waves the banks of the Marne.[3]

(ll. 151-62)

The suffering inflicted by war extends beyond the battlefield to strike cities and churches; theft, rape, and death strike the countryside. These passages form a curiously tragic and unconscious forecast of the condition of France several years later when Ronsard will write his discourses on the miseries of France in the throes of civil war. In contrast to this grim picture, he urges his fellow citizens to seek the divine blessings of Peace, the ministering spirit of God, who brings order from chaos, accompanied by industry and plenty.

The return of peace and the accompanying festivities, public rejoicings, and royal marriages are celebrated in several long poems. The theme announced in the *Exhortation pour la Paix* is continued in *La Paix, au Roy*, which in turn was followed by a separate poem to celebrate the return of the Lord Constable Montmorency from captivity. To Henri II Ronsard says that history will record the conquests and the defeats of his reign, but more important than these, it will tell of peace. The myth of Peace bringing order from chaos is once again stated, this time followed by a warning. When men have deserved divine punishment for their misdeeds, signs appear, warning of the impending outbreak of violence and war. The description of these protents and the ensuing violence is once again an uncanny prophecy of coming events. To this violence Ronsard opposes love, which holds all creation together:

> But why trifle with such petty themes
> When the stars of heaven, and all the scaly dwellers
> Within the sea, the great monsters of the deep,
> All that lives in earth, and the airy birds
> Which, hanging in the air, float upon the winds,
> All are filled with love and sustained by it.
>
> (*La Paix, au Roy,*
> ll. 177-82)

Without this sustaining love, Discord reigns. Even kings would do well to avoid violence and forbear to tempt Fortune, always untrustworthy, as Henri II has himself found:

> What more do you wish? Fortune is fickle,
> You yourself have found in honorable trials.
> It is enough, enough. It is time henceforth
> To trample war to earth and speak of it no more.
> Do you think you are God? The world's honor passes,
> And whatever one does, one day he must die,
> And after your death, though you were Emperor,
> You shall be no greater than a simple peasant.
>
> (ll. 229-36)

Thus Ronsard, drawing on the ancient themes of the mutability of Fortune and the equality of all men in death, warns the king that he shares in the common fate of all men. These are not the words of a fawning courtier. Commonplaces they may be, but Ronsard felt the need of restating them for his generation. His poem ends with an eloquent and moving prayer to Peace, "great daughter of God."

In all these poems, and in the welcome to the Lord Constable Montmorency, the spokesman of the peace party in the Council, one senses the immense relief of a people longing for peace and the public display of elation at its proclamation. The populace welcomes its hero returning from captivity like an infant, deprived of its nurse and restored to her. Thus France rejoices:

> Rise up, France, rise up, and lustily set about
> Lighting in the crossroads bonfires of joy;

> Let the wine flow freely and the people heartily
> Rejoice in dancing all about the bonfires.
> Let chaplets of flowers crown their heads
> And the day of his return be feasted forever.
> (*La Bienvenue de Monseigneur
> le Connestable,* ll. 59-64)

This joy was tragically short-lived. The sudden death of Henri II, killed accidentally in a tournament celebrating the royal weddings which sealed the peace, put an end to the festivities and to the uneasy peace between rival houses and rival creeds. Within months the country was plunged from festival into stark tragedy in one of those sudden pendulum swings which mark the history of France.

III *Catholic Poet: Elegies and Discours on the Civil-Religious Wars*

In his odes, hymns, and longer poems addressed to Henri II, Ronsard had already begun to fulfill the role of the poet-prophet, the *vates*, whose duty and calling it was to admonish and advise the ruler and his subjects. For Charles IX, the young king for whom he was to feel the deepest personal attachment and loyalty. Ronsard composed an *Institution,* a kind of poetic instruction and catechism. Following the humanistic tradition of Erasmus and Luis Vives, he advised the young monarch on his public duties and private life, both in regard to general conduct and personal behavior.[4]

We are not surprised to note that these poems often express the policies of the Queen Regent, Catherine de Medici and her chancellor, L'Hospital. This policy was one of pacification through compromise and tolerance; its aim was to reconcile the hostile parties, both dynastic and religious. Opposing it were the Protestants, led by members of the Bourbon-Condé family and the Colignys; and the militant Catholics, whose principal leaders were the Duc de Guise and his brother, the Cardinal de Lorraine. Between the two extremes were the majority of the French, loyal to church and crown, still for a time following the lead of the moderates, the *politiques.* To this middle group Ronsard generally gave allegiance, though during the bitter fighting of 1562-69 he tended to side with the more militant Catholics, at one time taking up arms to defend his benefice against Protestant marauders.

We can follow the events of these years through Ronsard's poems. The first to deal with the growing disorders is his *Discours à Guillaume des Autels* (published in 1560). In this rather long poem Ronsard discusses the need of the Catholics to defend their cause against the books and pamphlets of the Protestants, who have beguiled the credulous populace. (In a revision of 1562, Ronsard called for armed repression; later he restored his first version.) According to Ronsard, both Protestants and Catholics have erred. Against the Protestants he draws up a list of charges: sedition against the crown; false pride in presuming to upset customs hallowed by age and substituting those of foreigners; defamation of those in authority (a reference to attacks on the Guises); arrogance in presuming to be sole possessors of the truth and condemning the entire Roman Church. Likewise he brings charges against the Catholic clergy, mostly relating to neglect of the hierarchy to perform their duties, from the papacy down, to scandalous and worldly lives, and to greed and debauchery. Obviously the Church needs reform. Now, Ronsard says, France is torn asunder by her own children and is falling a prey to foreigners. Her sufferings had indeed been foretold in the book of Nostradamus and by signs and portents, all of which Ronsard firmly believed. Only the vigorous action of the Guises has saved the country from anarchy and heresy. (This is a reference to the brutal suppression of the conspiracy of Amboise.) For their well-being Ronsard offers a closing prayer.

This is the first publication in which Ronsard clearly takes a stand in the civil-religious controversies which were finally coming into the open. With friends and protectors in both camps he had been understandably hesitant. Now the lines were drawn. Ronsard, a Catholic churchman and a royal poet, chose to remain true to the faith of his ancestors and loyal to his king.

In this *Discours* can be found many of the themes which are prominent in the greater poems of 1562-63: the failures of both sides in the religious dispute are clearly stated and the premonition of the disasters of sedition and violence drawn in dark colors. The poet makes a strong plea for loyalty and patriotism. The strong language, direct and conversational, is heightened by rhetorical structures and devices; the skill with which Ronsard sets forth ideas, and the overtones of polemic and satire, are already noticeable.

In his *Elegie à Lois des Masures* (published in 1560) Ronsard seems to be writing an apology for the mixed nature of his books of *Poëmes*, which this epistle concludes. After explaining the nature of this collection Ronsard turns to answer his Protestant critics, who, he says, claim that his poetry is the depraved writing of one led astray by the Devil. In his answer to these critics Ronsard reveals for the first time his superb gifts as a satirist.

> Oh poor deluded souls, deceived by pride
> To think yourselves far wiser than the Church!
> Keep your shirts on, and judge no man;
> I am what I am, my conscience is clear,
> And God, to Whom all hearts are open,
> Knows my will and sounds it out.
>   Oh truly blessed Lorrainers, whom Calvin's sect
> And the errors of lands near by your own
> Never have misled: how came the spirit
> To stir a wind-bag German, locked in a hot room,
> To explicate so well the holy scriptures
> Among the tankards, wines, and oaths?

> (*Elegie à Lois Des Masures*,
> ll.43-54)

The two paragraphs reveal Ronsard as already a master of controversy and polemic satire. His control of the colloquial style within a formal rhetorical frame is perfect. The exclamations of pity and scorn, the advice to critics to mind their business ("Tenez vous en vos peaux"), and the paraphrase of Scripture for his personal justification form a swift and telling reply to the Huguenot critics. In contrast to these Huguenots are the inhabitants of Lorraine, the province of the Guise family, addressed in the second paragraph. These blessed souls have never been seduced into following new doctrines contrived by "un poussif Allement" (Luther) who is drawn in true caricature style as a drunkard closeted in an overheated stoveroom, surrounded by the gross debauchery of a Teutonic tavern.

After this outburst Ronsard tells his correspondent of a dream in which the ghost of du Bellay appeared to him.[5] The ghastly apparition is described in macabre detail with all the horrors of the realistic funeral monuments of the late Middle Ages and Renaissance. In a long prosopopoea du Bellay advises Ronsard to stay firm in his Christian faith and to shun the temptations of worldly ambitions:

As for thy world, it is a vain chimera,
Thy harsh bedlam, and not thy gentle mother:
There all is ruled by fortune and by whim,
There nothing lasts in perfect unity.
God changes not; man is naught but smoke
Kindled for a day by a tiny spark.

(ll. 101-6)

Ronsard is advised to avoid fame and to live in seclusion:

If thou give belief to the spirits of the dead
Which are no longer false, withdraw, Ronsard,
Live in thy house alone, and now grey haired,
Cease to serve the court, thy tempting Circe.

(ll. 111-14)

This advice, unheeded by Ronsard, might have spared him future disappointments. But by ignoring it Ronsard remained bound to the court and became its chief spokesman, critic, and entertainer.

Despite the severe measures of the Guise family and their partisans, despite the attempts at reconciliation made by the Queen Regent Catherine de Medici and her Chancellor Michel de L'Hospital, the signs of civil-religious war seemed clearer than ever: mass killings, followed by reprisals; negotiations with foreign princes; clashes in the cities and towns all over the kingdom. The Estates-General met at Orléans (1560-61), then at Pontoise near Paris to seek reforms and settle disputes. A public debate between Catholic and Protestant theologians was arranged at Poissy by the Queen Mother. The meeting, which began with some signs of hope, ended in acrimonious discord. (Ronsard, who was present, repeats in later poems some of the arguments advanced for the Catholic cause by the Cardinal of Lorraine.) The Duc de Guise and his men, passing through the town of Vassy, precipitated the massacre of Protestants worshiping in a barn (March 1562); several weeks later he entered Paris as a triumphant hero. The Protestants, led by Condé and members of the Bourbon family, and by Coligny, took up arms and demanded satisfaction. Soon Orléans, Angers, Tours, and Blois were in their hands. In the South priests and monks were slaughtered by the populace. In Sens, Tours, and Angers hundreds of Protestants were killed and their bloody corpses thrown into rivers. In the western provinces, Touraine and Anjou, bands of Protestants smashed statues, pillaged churches, destroyed relics, and desecrated the tombs of kings and nobles. The gloomy prophecies of Nostradamus and the baleful stars had been fulfilled.

These are the events which inspired the composition of Ronsard's *Discours sur les Misères de ce temps, à la Royne Mère*. This is no longer an epistle; the tone is already more lofty, the conviction more forceful, the imagery more vivid. Ronsard urges the Queen Mother to take firm hold of the ship of state and save it from the storm, and the entire kingdom joins in his plea. Urging it also are generations of the kings of France who have built the fair patrimony now a prey of the seditious and the foreigner.

Here Ronsard introduces the allegorical figure of Opinion, "the plague of human kind." She is the daughter of Jupiter and Dame Presumption, a monster brought up by Pride, Fantasy, and Wild Youth; hiding in her gown is Ambition. Having entered the studies of foreign theologians "these strange new Rabbis" and thoroughly confused them, she urges them to equal the audacity of the Giants and to seek to scale the Heavens. Discord then spreads to France, where all order and authority is overturned.

This allegory, severely condemned by most of Ronsard's critics, is certainly "artificial." But it is well in keeping with his poetic practice and that of his time.[6] In any case, the passage is brief enough, and the following scenes of discord, anarchy, and violence (ll. 159-96), the most direct and moving in the poem, gain in effect after this allegorical introduction.

Ronsard's *Discours*, apparently written at the request of the queen and the chancellor, had little immediate effect. Desperate to prevent the open war which threatened between the two armed camps, Catherine de Medici held several conferences in the summer of 1562, seeking to conciliate the militant Protestants led by the Prince de Condé and Admiral Coligny. In the provinces sporadic outbursts of violence increased in ferocity, incited by inflammatory pamphlets, the best of them written by Protestants. This was the state of affairs when Ronsard composed his *Continuation* of the previous discourse (August-October, 1562).

The circumstances of the composition and Ronsard's own convictions explain the passion, intensity, and satire of the sequel. The opening passage sets the tone of patriotism and indignation which mark the poem:

> Madam, I would be made of lead or of wood
> If I, who by nature was born a Frenchman,
> Did not tell for ages yet to come the grief
> And the dire misfortune with which our France is filled.
> I wish, despite the time, to proclaim to the world
> With an iron pen upon paper of steel
> That her own sons have seized and stripped her
> And basely beaten her even unto death.
>
> *(Continuation . . ., ll. 1-28)*

Then, just as in the earlier poem, Ronsard turns to the Protestants and charges them with pride and hypocricy. To these charges he adds the offenses of violence and sedition, vandalism and sacrilege:

> And so these fine braggarts, the feigned sons of God
> In their right hand bear a sword, in the other fire,
> And like madmen who rave and slaughter
> Sack the cities and strip the sacred temples.
> What! to burn houses, to pillage and steal,
> To kill, assassinate, command by force,
> No more obey the King, to build up armies,
> Is that what you call the Church Reformed?
>
> (ll. 41-48)

After a long series of similes between the Protestants and the locusts of the Apocalypse (ll. 71ff.), Ronsard addresses his former friend Theodore de Bèze, once a humanist and poet, now second only to Calvin as leader of the Reformed Church of Geneva. Bèze had been the chief Protestant theologian to address the Colloquy of Poissy. During his stay in Paris he had been seen there and in the suburbs at the turbulent "preachings" described later by Ronsard. First Ronsard tells him that the armed men raised up by his seditious sermons will die like the earthmen born of the dragon's teeth. Then, in a moving and direct appeal to Bèze's feelings for his homeland he adds:

> De Bèze, this is not some Gothic land,
> Some wilderness of Tartars, or of Scyths,
> It is your native land, which sweetly welcomed thee
> When at Vezelay thy mother conceived thee,
> The land which nurtured thee, and taught thee
> From thy tender youth science and the arts
> To do her service, and not for base abuse.
>
> (ll. 107-14)

Ronsard urges Bèze to repay his debt to France by calling off the armed troups ready to fight:

> Preach no more in France a Gospel of arms,
> A pistol-packing Christ blackened with smoke
> Wearing on his head a helmet, and in his hand
> A great cutlass red with human blood.
>
> (ll. 119-22)

Rather than this outrage, Bèze would do well to return to the profane pursuits of his youth.

Next Ronsard gives us one of those vignettes with which his long poems are studded: escorted by the troups of Condé, dressed in a long German cavalry cloak, a sword at his side, Bèze harangues the congregation outside the gates of Paris. At Ronsard's objections to Bèze's "message," two of the armed congregation accuse him of atheism for rejecting "this holy prophet sent by the Lord." This gives Ronsard the opening for a long reply in which the poet uses all the arms of satire and eloquence to ridicule and condemn the beliefs and practices of the new sect. Here he is more detailed and more caustic than in earlier poems; he becomes in turn indignant, ironic, and directly scornful. The Protestants are frauds, preaching one thing, practicing another; they have rejected the Fathers of the Church, but claim to follow the prophets of the Old Testament. In reality they have introduced murder and treason. (The charge of treason to the crown was the most difficult for them to answer and the one accusation which most damaged their cause.) Even among themselves they disagree and wrangle. (This is the greatest argument employed by Catholic apolgists.)

After a brief supplication for Condé and his dear patron Odet de Coligny and a prayer for their conversion, Ronsard introduces the allegorical figure of France. Her scepter shaken, her royal robe of fleurs-de-lis torn, she explains the reason for her condition. From Geneva, a mutinous city, has come her misfortune; she is now torn in pieces by her own people. Her language is moving, and expressed in the strongest metaphors. In her mouth the condition of the whole land becomes a great dirge for an ancient heritage trampled underfoot.[7]

The most eloquent, and by far the longest of the three poems on the civil-religious wars was written shortly before the first battle of the civil war at Dreux. The *Remonstrance au Peuple de France*, as its title indicates, is not addressed to the Queen Mother but to the entire nation. Each estate (the judges and magistrates are considered as a "second estate") is called upon to return to its loyalty and to perform the duties of its place.

After an opening prayer to God in which Ronsard calls down divine retribution upon the heads of the heretics and rebels, he notes that the conflict of Christians would puzzle and outrage an infidel, as it in fact disgusts Ronsard. Without his faith in the religion of his birth he would indeed prefer some ancient cult:

> At night I should adore the beams of the Moon,
> At dawn the Sun, the common light of all,
> The eye of the world; for if God have eyes
> The beams of the sun are his radiant eyes,
> Giving life to all, sustaining and guiding us
> And beholding the deeds of the people of earth.
> I say, that great Sun who gives us Seasons
> As he enters or as he leaves his twelve houses,
> Who fills the whole world with his renowned strength,
> Who with a wink of his eyes scatters the clouds,
> The spirit, the soul of the world, ardent, flaming,
> Circling the whole Heaven in his daily course,
> Full of vast grandeur, round, moving, and fixed,
> Who has for his borders the whole world below,
> Resting, restless, idle, and never still,
> The eldest son of Nature, the father of day.

> (*Remonstrance au People de France*,
> ll. 63-78)

We recognize in this magnificent hymn to the sun the author of the *Hymnes* of 1555-56 and the poet who published shortly after the first peace of Amboise (1563) his collection of four hymns of the seasons. Here, too, we find one of the passages in Ronsard's poetry which appealed to Montaigne, who cites it in *Essais* II, 13. Like Ronsard, Montaigne, in the opening section of his *Apologie de Raymond Sebond* (*Essais* II, 12), pointed to the scandal of fratricidal conflicts and barbarous cruelty between supposed Christains.

Ronsard's attitude toward faith and tradition was likewise appealing to Montaigne. Basically it is fideism, a blind trust and belief in mysteries beyond the competence of feeble human reason and understanding.

> It is right to dispute over natural things,
> Over lightning, winds, snows and frost,
> But not over faith, which we must not doubt.
> We must only believe, and not dispute.

> (ll. 143-46)

For God, the hidden God, does not wish His secrets searched out by the weak and erring minds of men. Yet the "new Doctors" of the various Protestant groups do this, despising tradition, perverting the minds of the simple who in turn believe they are experts in theology. Anyone, by adopting these new ways, can become a "new theologian."

> One must only with great temerity
> Detest the Papacy, speak against the Mass,
> Be modest in his speech, with long beard,
> A furrowed forehead, his eyes wild and deep,
> His hair unkempt, a scowling brow, a pallid face,
> Appear but seldom, compose many a tract
> Speak of Jehovah, the Lord, the Christ,
> Cover his shoulders with a long German cloak,
> In short, be a cut-throat and swear only "Yea."
> (ll. 195-204)

This is certainly one of the first, and one of the best, satires of the new "puritans" whose ways of behavior Ronsard thought ridiculous and hypocritical.[8]

Opinion, the allegorical monster from the *Continuation des Misères*, appears again in a much more elaborate passage showing her terrible progress. With the insistence of a drum beat, Ronsard introduces her devastations with *De là* . . . . These may be the punishment of the laxness of French Catholics, who are again urged to reform themselves. Ronsard calls upon all the estates of the kingdom to serve the crown, and last of all on the poets, "sacred darlings of the Muses." A final outburst of indignation builds to a mounting crescendo of rage (each introduced by "Je meurs quand le voi . . ."). Then, turning to the royal army he addresses them in stirring words of encouragement and concludes with a prayer to God for vengeance.

These poems are certainly masterpieces of polemic and of patriotic and poetic eloquence. Nor are they lacking in clarity of expostulation and in incisive, if occasionally unfair, attacks on the enemies of the Church. Soon Ronsard was the target of virulent personal attacks by Protestant pamphleteers. They follow the tradition of the humanist invective in prose or verse; no matter is too personal, no half-truth too doubtful to be flung into print.

Ronsard's reply, one of his longest poems, is a full apology for his position and a scathing counterattack. The rambling title gives an idea of this equally long and rambling poem: *Responce de P. de Ronsard Gentilhomme Vandômois, aux injures et calomnies de ie ne sçay quels Predicans & Ministres de Genève*. Regretting that he must skirmish, not with Bèze himself, but with some second-rate versifiers, Ronsard nevertheless sets about his defense with relish, displaying as he goes his own learning, superiority in poetry and confidence in defending his position.

The poem is far too long for detailed study. The most interesting passages seem to me those in which Ronsard exorcises the madness of the Protestant poet turned into a werewolf (ll. 129-210), the account of his own life in the country, and a defense of his poetry.

The *apologia pro vita sua* (ll. 513-600) is a rare and precious document on Ronsard's life and tastes as well as a notable example of his sustained middle style in poetry, so natural and yet so rich in detail and full of movement. After spending his mornings over his books, he tells his critic, he has dinner ("a sober repast") and goes out for recreation:

> For if the afternoon is pleasant and calm
> I go off for a walk, now in a meadow,

> Now in a village, and now in a wood,
> Now through solitary and quiet haunts.
> I love those gardens which savor of the wild,
> I love the stream which gurgles on the bank.
>
> (*Responce . . .*, ll. 531-36)

He chats with a friend, falls asleep in a clump of flowers, or propped against a willow, he reads. In a curious four-line passage (later carefully removed) he candidly admits his taste for pleasure unbecoming a cleric and scandalous to the Calvinists:

> I like to make love, I like speaking to ladies,
> To put into writing my amorous flames;
> I like balls, dancing, and masquerades as well,
> Music and the lute, the enemies of care.
>
> (*Responce . . .* ll. 551-54)

Unlike his critics, he is not bent on conversions by violence. But when he must fulfill his duties as canon of St. Julien at Le Mans he is, like Rabelais' Frère Jean, "a clerk to the teeth."

The other apology, for his poetry, is equally interesting (ll. 847-928; 1001-42). The Protestant critic has accused Ronsard's muse of disorder and confusion, expressed by Ronsard in an extended simile of the threshing floor and the winnower. But the critic is simply dull and is unable to perceive the art in poetry. Truly inspired, Ronsard's poetry does not, like a sermon, follow logical but poetic order. It remains hidden from mere versifiers. The true poet, Hesiod, Pindar, Horace, or Tibullus, gathers his nectar at random among the flowers.[9] The dull, serious, pedantic critic is unable to follow the free play and elegant folly of this noble poetry. After a long digression Ronsard returns to his claim to the laurel crown and once again he gives a poetic autobiography (ll. 1011-26). But this time it is followed by a note of regret which will be sounded with variations in his old age: his gift to France has been misused, this time by heretics, later by a crowd of silly versifiers. Then he turns on his critic:

> Thou cannot deny it! for with my plenty
> You are filled: I am your only model,

You have all come from my greatness,
You are my subjects, and I am your law.

(*Responce* . . . , ll. 1035-38)

And he was right. Not only did the Protestant poets follow his lead as the premier poet of France, but almost all French poets well into the following century are his offspring. And in a wider sense, so is the loftiest French poetry of all centuries since.

CHAPTER 8

The Poet of Charles IX

I Poetry on Commission

THE poems written during the outbreak of the civil-religious wars are proportionately a small part of the vast number of works composed by Ronsard at the request of the court, or at the request of courtiers. The *Discours* and *Remonstrance* stand out from many of the court poems largely because of the intensity of feeling expressed in a vigorous and highly vivid style. In many other works Ronsard was forced to conform to an occasion, or to follow the conventional style of expression in vogue in court circles or in the salons of Paris. Though these poems written at the request of king or noble are often the least interesting of Ronsard's work, they too bear the stamp of his genius at times and are not without merit.

The role of *poëte courtisan* so haughtily despised by the young "Brigade" was a source of both pride and vexation to Ronsard. So long as he could appear as counsellor, prophet, or seer he might feel pride in continuing the tradition of Pindar, or of Horace in his Roman odes. But the Renaissance court demanded less exalted poems and paintings from its artists-in-residence. Leonardo da Vinci, Ariosto, and Michelangelo had not been above providing stage settings and scenarios for court festivals. Nor was Ronsard absent from the list of poets who decorated triumphal arches, threw down a challenge (*cartel*) in verse for a tourney, or rhymed sonnets, madrigals, and elegies for a royal or noble suitor. Beginning in 1559, and throughout the reign of Chales IX, Ronsard became in fact as well as in name *Poëte du Roy*.

The most prolific period of Ronsard's production of court verse is indeed the rule of Charles IX, who was devoted to his poet. The *Recueil de Trois Livres de Nouvelles Poësies* (1563) parallels in composition the great *Discours* and reveals a Ronsard still occupied with sonnets, madrigals, and even more with the elegy, a form which is often closer to the epistle than to a lament. Following the peace of Amboise (1563) and the attempts of the Queen Regent to pacify the kingdom by entertainments at court and tours of the provinces, Ronsard was called upon to further the royal policy by providing poems for all sorts of festivities at Fontainebleau, Bar-le-Duc, and later for the great meeting of the queen of Spain with her French royal relatives at Bayonne. These make up most of the poems published in *Elegies, Mascarades et Bergerie* (1565) dedicated to Elizabeth of England. Later, as they returned to Paris, the young king and his mother paid Ronsard the honor of a personal visit to the priory at St. Cosme-lès-Tours, which his importunate poetic compliants had finally obtained. There the poet presented his royal master with a gift of melons from his garden accompanied by delightful sonnets.[1] And there the young king may once again have encouraged Ronsard to take up his abandoned epic, this time writing in the ten-syllable line of the older French poems.

With the possibility of retreating from the court to his two priories of Croixval in Anjou and Saint Cosme in Touraine, Ronsard began the continual return and retreat which would mark his life until his final retirement from the court. He was drawn to Paris as the center of his intellectual life and the home of many friends and to court because he still required patronage. It was during his stay in Paris or at court that many of the commissioned poems in the following decade were composed.

During this time Ronsard was busy not only with poems for the court but for courtiers as well. His friends had already reproached him for selling his Muse to the powerful and great for favors. The Protestant critics did not fail to add this fault to their list of sins thrown in his teeth. And in spite of his haughty reply to them one senses that this thrust was close to the quick, for in spite of his efforts to appear independent and to hide the evidence in his work, Ronsard did indeed "rent his Muse" if only to the very highest bidders.

Among the more important collections "hammered out on the order of the Great" are the sonnets for Mlle Limeuil; a number of elegies and sonnets composed for the love affairs of the Prince de Condé; and a collection of poems celebrating the infatuation of Charles IX for Anne d'Acquaviva, *Les Amours d'Eurymedon et de Callirée* (published in 1578).

A special group of poems, skillfully incorporated into the fabric of *Amours II* has already been mentioned: these are the poems entitled *Sur la Mort de Marie*. Critics have unanimously accepted the discovery that they were written originally as part of a poetic "tomb" for the young mistress of Henri III, Marie de Bourbon, Princesse de Clèves.[2] By adroit changes and clever suppression of details, Ronsard has managed to adapt most of the poems to the central theme which was the motif of the new *Amours II*: Marie the "simple peasant lass" from Anjou. Readers who know the famous sonnet "Comme on voit sur la branche au mois de mai la rose . . . " only as an anthology piece are likely to be unaware of its probable origin and untroubled by how inappropriate its descriptions are for a peasant woman who, in 1578, was long since past her "première jeunesse."

As has been noted, the mere fact that a work of art was executed on commission does not always imply a callous lack of feeling on the part of the artist. We are still touched by the sonnet on the death of Marie, just as we are moved by many works of Renaissance artists or by the music of Mozart, all done on commission. While it is true that many of the love poems written to order by Ronsard suffer from a facility and a certain abstract conventional language, even banality, many of them bear traces of his talent and genius. But they are rarely among his finest, or even average works.

Poetry was always for Ronsard something more than an entertainment for kings and princes (though he had thus defined it in his cavalier fashion to his Huguenot critics), and one can find in the court poems sonnets and passages from longer works which may well be placed among Ronsard's finer creations. Among them I have chosen the elegies to Mary Stuart, the *Bergerie* for the festival at Fontainebleau, and the *Tombeau de Marguerite de France*.

II *Poems for Mary Queen of Scots*

The figure of Mary Stuart, Queen of France and Scotland, has never entirely lost the charm which the young princess cast over the French court. Ronsard, who had served as a page at her father's court at Edinburgh, saw her frequently as she grew under the tutelage of her Guise uncle into the loveliest and most gifted of the royal children. As wife of François II she had been briefly queen of France. Diplomatic rapprochement with England and dynastic jealousy led Catherine de

Medici to send her back to Scotland. Her departure was the occasion of several poems in Ronsard's *Recueil* of 1563-64.

In the first elegy Ronsard shows France as a garden stripped of its loveliest flower, as a heaven without stars. Always pursued by malignant Fortune the unhappy princess must leave for her island:

> No more nor less than in a flowery garden
> Dies the fair lily, when heavy rain
> Weighs down its drooping head,
> Or when at evening the rose's color fades,
> And parched, it dies, when heat
> Drinks the moisture which gave it life
> And leaf by leaf, fading, it falls.

> > (*Elegie sur le depart de la Royne d'Escosse*, "Comme un beau pré depouillé de ses fleurs . . . ," Laum. XII, 193-99. ll. 34-40)

His sorrow at her departure is equal only to his grief at losing Marguerite de France, now Duchesse de Savoie. No higher tribute could be paid the lovely young queen who sang Ronsard's poems to her own accompaniment.

The second elegy, written after the queen had sailed for Scotland, shows the same vessel bearing away the Muses and the inspiration of French poets. In a long single sentence, a threnody made of questions, Ronsard asks what the poets will sing of when all the queen's beauty, grace, and charm have gone:

> When that white ivory swelling your breast,
> When your fair and long and delicate hand
> When your fair frame and your fair heart,
> Which seemed the portrait of a divine Image . . .
have gone,
> How could the mouths of Poets sing,
> When at your departure the Muses are mute?

> > (*Elegie à la Royne d'Escosse*, "Le jour que vostre voyle aux vagues se courba . . . ," Laum. XII, 277-84. ll. 33-36; 43-44)

This portrait of the queen and the white delicacy of her beauty are the theme of the most beautiful of the poems composed by Ronsard for Mary Stuart. Though the memory of the queen's lovely face is stamped forever on Ronsard's heart, he has a further remembrance, her portrait in which she wears the flowing white robes of French court mourning. No jewels detract from the whiteness of her hand, the delicacy of her fingers or her breast:

> A long, delicate and flowing crepe
> Fold after fold, twisted and turned,
> Mourning dress, is your cover
> From your head to your waist,
> Swelling like a sail, when the wind
> Blows on the ship, urging it ahead.
> In such dress you were attired
> Leaving, alas, the fair country
> Whose Sceptre you once held,
> When pensive, and bathing your breast
> With the fair crystal of streaming tears
> Sadly you went through the long walks
> Of the garden of that royal castle
> Which takes its name from a spring.
>   All the gardens whiten neath your veils
> As on the mast one sees the sails grow white
> And curve, billowing over the sea
> When the slaves have stopped their rowing:
> And the galley, pushed at the whim of the wind,
> Wave upon wave, goes plunging ahead
> Plowing the sea, and with a great roar
> Pirouetts the wave following in its wake.

> *(Elegie*, "Bien que le trait de vostre
> belle face . . .," Laum. XIV, 152-59, ll. 19-40)

III *Mascarade, Pastoral, Eclogue, Ballet: The* Bergerie

The most ambitious work in the collection dedicated to Elizabeth of England is the *Bergerie* of 1565. Composed for the festivals of Fontainebleau[3] in the early spring of 1564, the *Bergerie* follows the prose epistle to Elizabeth and a fulsome elegy to her favorite, Lord Dudley ("Mylord Robert Du-Dlé, comte de l'Encestre"). This royal entertainment is dedicated to Elizabeth's rival, Mary Queen of Scots, who, as has been noted, was still much in the mind of Ronsard. Like many of Ronsard's other eclogues it follows the Renaissance pastoral conventions in allotting rustic names to members of the court and in adopting the Vergilian bucolic setting to contemporary events.[4]

The *Bergerie*, however, differs from other eclogues in its elaborate setting and in the presence of soloists and chorus for prologue and epilogue as well as in the designation in names of characters of the noble children for whom the five major roles were intended. It was, as Laumonier notes, "a kind of mascarade-pastoral or eclogue-ballet" probably with provision for musical setting, lavish costuming, and dancing; in brief, the very sort of Italianate entertainment which became the hallmark of the Valois court and was to be renewed with brilliant success at the Bourbon court of the seventeenth century. It may well have been the forerunner of the English court masque.

The Prologue presents the rustic setting and introduces the "noble shepherds"; it is followed by a double chorus emerging from two caves singing in alternating lyric verses the praise of Catherine de Medici, who had arranged the festivities as a means of creating a diversion for the warring nobility. The combined choruses then join in praise of Carlin (Charles IX).

We are next introduced to the principal actors who will deliver the main portion of the poem in their roles as shepherds: Orléantin, Duc d'Orléans, the future Henri III; Angelot, François, Duc d'Anjou, his younger brother; Navarrin, his cousin Henri de Navarre, the future Henri IV; Guisin, Henri, Duc de Guise; and Margot, Marguerite de Valois, the king's sister. The oldest of these actors, Henri de Guise, was only thirteen; the youngest, Anjou, only nine.

Orléantin, after describing a conventional but quite convincing spring setting, proposes a singing contest among the shepherds. Each of the young shepherds in turn offers a prize to be given the winner. The description of the prizes offers Ronsard the occasion for the elaborate descriptive poetry so much enjoyed by his contemporaries and obviously a favorite tour de force of the poet. Orléantin offers a tame deer, Angelot a goat. Navarrin's prize is a wooden vessel carved "with great artifice" and painted with a mythological scene of the kind found on the elegant mannerist *objets d'art* of the period often described in Ronsard's earlier odes and poems. In the center of the composition a satyr is seizing a shepherdess:

> Her kerchief is falling, and in every way
> Her lovely hair blows at the wind's mercy;
> Whereupon she, angered and ardent in her heart,
> Turns her face away from the satyr,
> Struggles to escape, and with her right hand
> Tears the hair from his chin and chest,
> And with her left she flattens his nose.
> But in vain; for ever the Satyr is master.
>   Three children, with arms and legs bare,
> Modeled after nature, ever plump and fat,
> Are carved round about; one with lively effort
> Seeks to force the Satyr to let go his prey,
> And with childish hand twice or thrice
> Taking the goatish hand, opens it out.
> The other, fiercer still, with his sharp tooth
> Bites the ravisher god on his hairy thigh,
> Presses on his leg, and pinches him so hard
> That blood gushes out from beneath his nails,
> And signals the third child to come to his aid.
> But the other boy, begged all in vain,
> Bending over, draws a thorn from his foot
> As he sits on a lawn of green pimpernel,
> Paying no heed to him who calls.

(Bergerie, ll. 185-208)

Such lavish detail devoted to every motion and gesture, such exact and "artificial" realism in the sophisticated rendering of an apparently popular subject, shows Ronsard's verbal kinship with the plastic as well as the poetic art of Hellenistic times and the highly wrought and detailed artifacts so much in vogue during his own time, now referred to as mannerism.

After the other shepherds have offered their prizes, the contest begins. The recent civil wars have left their scars on the countryside, and this event is not absent from the apparently idyllic setting. The devastation of the wars is described movingly in the opening song by Orléantin (ll. 323-74). Though the vocabulary is pastoral throughout, as in Ronsard's model for this passage, the references to recent events are unmistakable: ". . . in short there was no place . . . however remote . . . Or rock so secret which had not felt the hand/And the barbarous voice of the greedy German" (ll. 357; 361-62).

Other contemporary events receive the attention of other singers: the pacification of the kingdom by Catherine de Medici; a long "deploration" and panegyric of the late King Henri II; a wistful recollection of the pleasure of the Golden Age (in contrast to the troubles of the recent past); a prophecy of the glories of the reign of Charles IX; and finally another "louange de France" which begins with one of Ransard's splendid passages addressed to the sun and moon. After all these pyrotechnics, the two speeches of shepherds which follow come as an anticlimax, but they merely serve to introduce the final appearance of the double chorus which provides the noble children, their king, and the audience with a series of moral quatrains on statecraft and ethics so much enjoyed by the Renaissance public. These quatrains, concluding a curious and strangely rich poem, give final lyric expression to much of the counsel expressed in Ronsard's earlier poems addressed to rulers.

Such is the *Bergerie*, a poem unique in the work of Ronsard, but containing many of the features associated with the conventional Renaissance pastoral and with much of the more ambitious verse composed by him for the court. It is not free of *longueurs*, but like many of his longer poems it is saved from triteness and banality by his supreme gifts of concrete metaphor and music together with a personal vision of the subjects imposed by custom.

IV *The* Franciade

"I know of few stories more disastrous than the fate of the *Franciade*. The ship cast off in a first outburst of enthusiasm, then the vessel stopped for lack of wind to swell the sails; when it resumed its journey, it was only to wander from sea to sea, tossed about by every storm, running upon every reef; it never reached port. The tribulations of this unfortunate poem were no less than those of its hero Francus."[5] Thus did Edmond Bourciez sum up the greatest failure of Ronsard's career. For the epic upon which the young Ronsard and his friends had set their hopes and aspirations was a disappointment to all his admirers. His efforts at revision, greater than for any other of his poems, are a sure sign of his own dissatisfaction. Despite them the poem as a whole is a failure.

It may well seem strange to find the *Franciade*, the four books of Ronsard's unfinished epic, discussed under the heading "court poetry."

And yet its unhappy history is closely bound with that of Ronsard's ambitions and disappointments at court. From his first sketch of the plot (1550) till its suspension at the death of Charles IX (1573) the poem depended upon the royal house whose legendary ancestor Francus, son of Hector, was the hero. Ronsard's poems of the 1550's and those of his fellow poets enable us to follow these ambitions, the poet's requests for support, his active propaganda at court and among his humanist colleagues, and his ultimate disillusions. As the quatrain composed by Ronsard's secretary Amadys Jamyn for the portrait of Charles IX testifies, the resumption of the abandoned epic in 1565 was undertaken at the king's command. Its verse form, the old ten-syllable line of the medieval epics, and the genealogical treatment of the French monarchs were his personal choice:

> Thou hast not, Ronsard, composed this work;
> It is forged by a royal hand.
> Charles, learned, victorious, and wise
> Is its author, thou only its writer.

Aside from the royal intervention in the composition of the poem, many reasons have been advanced for the poem's failure: Ronsard's insistence on a substantial pension from the crown and the repeated postponements of promised support at the time when his age and ambition most suited him to its composition; the king's interference in the final form of the poem; the choice of a subject which lacked historical verisimilitude and yet involved a long and tedious chronicle of the kings of France; Ronsard's own failure to follow his theory of the separation of fiction and history; the obvious subservience to an "epic formula" in the composition and arrangement of episodes. All these weaknessess may well have led Ronsard to abandon a project which could never have been successfully brought to a happy conclusion.[6]

If the *Franciade* is a failure as an epic poem and as an artistic whole, it is not without redeeming qualities, qualities one would expect from a familiarity with Ronsard's hymns, discourses, and *poëmes*. Throughout the four books one does find vivid and stirring scenes drawn from the world of nature observed directly by Ronsard and written of so often in Homer and Vergil, the two principal models of his poem. These passages occur most often in the extended similes or in the setting of important episodes. Ronsard's rereading of the ancient epics and the collaboration of Amadys Jamyn, who was finishing Hugues Salel's translation of Homer into French, provided him with the inspiration of many of these. Ironically it was the curse of the "epic formula" which doomed the poem as an entity but provided the inspiration of its finest passages.

Such passages occur in scenes and episodes throughout the four books, breaking the rather tiresome monotony of lengthy speeches and prophecies of the future hardships and final triumphs of Francus and his descendants. From Book I we might choose the feast of Cybele (ed. Laum ll. 393ff.), the building of Francus' fleet of ships (ll. 533-84) and their launching (ll. 585-608). In Book II we are given a bravura passage describing the inevitable tempest at sea and the wreck of the fleet. Both the building of the fleet and the storm at sea provide Ronsard with the opportunity to display in his vivid and concrete style his careful reading of the ancient epics as well as his own knowledge of the techniques of nautical construction and seamanship.

More interesting, perhaps, and certainly more typical of Ronsard himself, with his interest in the spirit world and his lifelong belief in ghosts and specters, is the appearance to Francus of the ghosts of his shipwrecked comrades begging for funeral rites. (Book II, ll. 641ff.; Laum. XVI, 125-26, Cohen, I, 690-91):

> While night in her star-studded robe
> Veiled the earth in thick shrouds
> With her dark mantle, shadowy and still,
> Then behold the fantoms of those
> Who by the great sea broken into waves
> Had been swallowed up, soul and body,
> Swollen, puffy, frothy with the waves,
> With noses eaten away, with frightful mien,
> Who, peeping in voices slow and long
> (Like little chicks seeking their lost mother)
> With hands and feet gesturing their fate,
> Surround the head of Francion.

> (ll. 641-52; text of 1584)

They then describe their drowning in the storm and their subsequent fate, condemned to wander the earth and sea until they receive proper funeral rites (ll. 653-76) described in the following passage:

> As soon as the roseate Aurora
> Had drawn the Sun from the water of ocean
> Francus arises, and with fresh sod
> Makes tombs, funereal dwellings,
> Then sprinkling from a great goblet full
> Sacred blood upon their empty tombs,
> He loudly calls down the souls who come
> And press thickly about the oblation,
> Making a sound such as, in their nest,
> Swallows make waiting to fill their beaks;
> And such as one sees (*sic*) in high summer
> In the brightest scorching light
> A wandering thick horde of trembling
> Mosquitos flying all together,
> Thick, yet tiny, whirling from place to place,
> And so small that they deceive the eyes.

(ll. 677-92)

This attention to details of sight, sound, and motion is characteristic of the similes drawn from nature, whether taken from ancient sources or combined with the personal observation of the poet. The *Franciade* abounds in such similes, perhaps the most attractive feature of the work. Some are quite brief, others extended and elaborate. In a later passage describing the fear of the two Cretan princesses who are watching Francus and the giant Phovere locked in mortal combat, the following simile occurs:

> But just as one sees two doves
> Shudder with fear under the cruel claws
> Of the sparrow-hawk, doves who had once
> Left their nest, and blithely were about
> To return to the dove-cote to give food
> To their dear children newly born,
> So trembled their hearts in their breasts . . .

(ll. 1332-39; Laum. XVI, 169; Coh. II, 705)

Later the story of the future kings of France, descendants of Francus, is shown to the hero in a vision conjured by the magician Hyante, one of the daughters of the hospitable king of Crete. After a sacrifice in the temple of Hecate (one of the finest passages of the entire poem) the priestess foretells the trials of Francus and shows him his progeny, the Merovingian kings from Pharamond to Pepin. Most critics, while admiring the satirical verse of the description of the "rois fénéants," captives of the mayors of the palace, find this chronicle tiresome. Professor Lebègue, who formerly shared this view, has more recently pointed out that, like so many other works of Ronsard composed for the Valois monarchs, this long passage contains moral lessons on the duties of kingship.[7] Each ruler is judged by posterity, and his example may be either a warning to avoid vices or an encouragement to follow his virtues. After a series of scathing portraits of vicious kings, interrupted occasionally to praise an exceptional ruler, the lazy and dull trio of Clothaire, Childeric, and Theodoric appear: "Three ne're-do-wells, great clods of dirt,/Neither good in peace, nor in time of war" (Book IV, ll. 1557-58). They are followed by slothful, sensual descendants, kings in name only: "Behold, Francion, three kings, conquered / By wine, by love, by sensualities . . . (IV, 1651-52). Through their vices and weakness the conquests of generations have been lost:

> Their fair kingdom, won by the harness
> Of many ancestors, invincible kings,
> By the sweat of many captains,
> By blood, by iron, by speech, by toil,
> Fallen in little time from its vigor,
> Ah! cruel fate! will lose strength and heart.

> (IV, ll. 1667-72)

Here we can clearly detect the accents of the poems on the civil wars and a warning (which went unheeded) to the Valois kings. This warning becomes more graphic with the description of the worthless and effeminate "rois fénéants," a description which could well have served as D'Aubigné's model for his satiric portrayal of the decadence of Henri III and his court:

> These hideous kings in long thick beards
> In long hair, adorned in strand after strand
> Of golden chains and graven carcanets,
> Raised high in a triumphal chariot
> Once each year will show their face.

> For all the rest, they'll be like serfs,
> Leaving the reins to Mayors of the Palace
> Whose slaves and varlets they will be,
> Masks of kings, animated statues,
> Not shepherds nor princes of armies,
> Who will be sullied by sensuality,
> Finally by their vassals overthrown.
> Learn, Trojan, how a cowardly heart
> Loses in a day its sceptre and its rank.
>
> (IV, ll. 1677-90)

This stillborn poem, Ronsard's greatest disappointment, is not a total failure. Unread today like most Renaissance epics, the *Franciade* holds in store for those few with the patience to cull them out, passages of great beauty, and a surprising variety of poetic scenes—sentimental, descriptive, dramatic, satiric, heroic. For most it will, as Ronsard predicted, remain a heavy burden.

V *Funeral Poems for the House of Valois*

Since his youth as a royal page Ronsard had been attached to the court, serving in succession the sons and daughters of François I. From 1554 he is referred to as "Poëte françois du Roy" and in 1559 he received the titles *conseiller* and *aumosnier ordinnaire du Roy.*

The death of Charles IX in 1574 and in the following year that of his aunt Marguerite de France, duchesse de Savoie, severed Ronsard's closest ties with the royal family. His affection for the king was real and deep and his feeling of admiration and his gratitude to Marguerite de France went back to his first years as a poet struggling for recognition.

Though he had addressed a number of complimentary poems to Charles's successor Henri III, the last of the Valois kings does not seem to have responded to these overtures. The king already had a favorite poet, the fashionable darling of the new court, Philippe Desportes. Ronsard, then, disillusioned with the fickleness of court favor and increasingly bitter at the shallowness of the young courtiers, retired to his priories, returning to Paris as a guest of the principal of the Collège de Boncourt and making only the rarest appearances at the Louvre. So although he didicated the *Bocage royal* in his great edition of 1584 to Henri III and wrote several important poems for him, and although Ronsard remained a royalist till his death, one may say that Ronsard's farewell to the house he had served so faithfully is contained in the funeral poems for Charles IX and for his aunt.

Though the poem in memory of the young king contains moving passages, the *Tombeau de Tres Illustre Princesse Marguerite de France* . . . with its 452 lines includes a history and lament for all the royal house from the sons of François I to the great princess whose name it bears. It is, in fact, a summation of Ronsard's career as a servant of that ill-starred house and is far more personal than the sort of poem usually written on such occasions. There are no passages which might be called great in this *Tombeau,* but one cannot fail to sense in it the accumulation of grief in this succession of youth, beauty, and grandeur, all cut off by death. These tragic stories of princes and kings were not commonplaces gathered from a book of rhetoric, but the incarnate testimony of the truth of those commonplaces, a truth repeatedly illustrated before Ronsard's eyes from his earliest youth until his own death. The feeling of personal loyalty, that of feudal vassal to lord, gives the *Tombeau* an immediate and moving sense of grief experienced and real. These emotions are occasionally heightened by rhetoric, but are nonetheless sincere. In the passage devoted to the reign of Charles IX we see the young king, barely ten, weeping from the heavy weight of the crown at his coronation, the first presage of a series of calamities which were to mark his reign:

> All rushed against him: the Sun, in its spite
> Loathing the Earth, dressed itself in black,
> Its face turned russet, and the silvery moon
> Long had its crescent splotched with bloody spots.
> The Seine beyond its banks unleashed its rage,
> Ceres the provider denied us her wheat,
> The good Father [Bacchus] his wines, and
> Pallas her leaves,
> And salt, so common, denied us his use:
> Famine and war and plague have shown
> That God in fury had come out against his folk.

> (Tombeau de Marguerite . . ., ll. 277-86)

Ronsard's imprecations against the nation are followed by a final tribute to his king whom "for fourteen years I served with Joy." He curses astrologers who predict the extinction of the Valois line. Then, as a culmination of grief, he gives a panegyric of Marguerite de France, his protectress at court, and patroness of learning and art. If he had the learning of the Romans, or the Muses of the Greeks, he says,

> I should say that just as the Eleusinian mother
> Sowed the fields with wheat, so she, entirely divine,
> The nursling of Helicon, sowed on every side
> In France trades, and learning, and arts:
> That she had a soul hospitable to the Muses . . .

(Tombeau, ll. 387-91)

At her elaborate imaginary obsequies Ronsard, dressed as Orpheus of old, will fulfill his debt of gratitude:

> [I shall] sing aloud in immortal tones
> The honor and favor humbly received from her,
> How she cared for me for the honor which I had
> Of serving her nephews, my masters and my Kings.
>   I shall tell that heaven is too envious of me
> To have me drag out so long a life
> And to hold in store for me a head half white
> To lament over the tombs of the Kings my providers.
>   I shall say that the life of the Great is unsure
> That foolish is the man who trusts the favor of the world
> A plaything of fortune, a flower of the spring,
> Since so many kings are seen to last so short a time.

(Tombeau, ll. 427-38)

The acceptance of the common fate of all marks this and the final address to Pibrac, Ronsard's friend, who perhaps weeps at the vanity of human greatness. The sadness of this poem, the tone of lament and bitter resignation which mark its conclusion are seldom absent from the more personal poems of Ronsard's last years.

CHAPTER 9

Ronsard's Private World

I *The* Sixiesme et Septiesme livres des Poëmes

IN all his poetic autobiographies, and in almost all his comments on poetry, Ronsard stresses the importance of retreat from the cares and anxieties of public life as a neccessity for the poet. Whether he is merely echoing his beloved ancients or stating a personal conviction, his descriptions of the solitary haunts inhabited by the Muses strike us as the most authentic passages from these poems. And as the poet grew older his own actions bear witness to his commitment to this withdrawal from the court and its useless bustle; Ronsard spent more and more of his time in his priories in Anjou and Touraine. We have already seen, in his reply to Protestant critics, what his life there was like in the early 1560's, and there is little reason to suppose that it changed much until his last sickness. There, surrounded by his books and the countryside in which he had grown to manhood, he revised and rearranged his earlier works for the great collected editions and composed some of his most personal poems. In them we catch a glimpse of his own feelings, his private life, the curious attachment which lead to his last great series of love poems, and his meditations on the human condition.

Among the fruits of Ronsard's long stay at his priories were the *Sixiesme et Septiesme Livres des Poëmes*, which are sequels to the miscellaneous category "poeme" arranged in five books in the edition of 1567. The sixth book is dedicated to Jean de Belot, a magistrate of Bordeaux and a great benefactor of Ronsard. Like earlier poems which describe such things as mistletoe, fine glass, or weapons—all written in appreciation of a gift from a former patron and friend—the opening poem is a *hymne-blason* (later entitled *La Lyre*) thanking Belot for the gift of an instrument sumptuously decorated with scenes from the legends of Apollo and the Gods.[1] Over half of the poem, however, is in the form of a personal letter to Belot in which Ronsard confides to his friend how his poetic inspiration had almost abandoned him, leaving him restless and bewildered. Then, encouraged by the friendship of Belot, Ronsard was once again visited by the divine frenzy, which he describes in some detail, giving us our clearest idea of how the poet felt when in the throes of composition. Though this description is filled with reminiscences of Plato and with elaborate similies, we sense that Ronsard is recounting his own experiences. (ll. 59-116). The praise of Belot's generosity then leads to the second part of the poem, the *hymne-blason* of Apollo and his instrument, whose scenes are presented in the same minute detail as the description of the carved goblet in the *Bergerie*.

Even more personal, and far more curious, is the *poëme* entitled *Le Chat*. It begins with a philosophical preamble on the spirit which animates the universe, a spirit which, however diverse its manifestations, inhabits all living creatures and the world in which they move.[2] Just as some men have a gift of prophecy, so certain creatures have been endowed with a similar power (ll. 43-58). From this general opening the poet then moves to his own experiences. Ronsard tells of a laurel tree which he had planted and carefully tended and of its sudden and mysterious wasting away at the hands of a malignant spirit; this he interprets as an omen of the quartan fever from which he was soon to suffer. His next warning is the kick of a horse, fatal to one of his servants, who kept his eyes fixed on his master at the moment of his death. "But above all," he continues, "the baleful Cat has a prophetic soul."

> Never lived a man in the world who hates
> Cats as I hate them with a deep hatred.
> I hate their eyes, their brow, and their glance:
> And, seeing them, I flee somewhere else,
> Trembling in every muscle, vein, and member;
> Never does a Cat enter my chamber,
> For I abhor all those who can not live
> Without a Cat which dwells close by;
> And nonetheless this hideous creature
> Came to lie quite close by my head
> Seeking the softness of a downy pillow

Where I was wont to sleep on my left side;
For it is my custom to sleep on my left
Till morning when the Cock awakens me.
   This Cat miaowed with a frightful cry,
I woke up with a start, out of my senses,
And jumping up I call to my servants . . .

(Le Chat, ll. 119-35)*

Thus, in this curious poem, which begins with a meditation on the *anima mundi* and contains lines of an almost pantheistic philosophy, we catch a glimpse of Ronsard at Croixval planting and tending his laurel tree, becoming anxious at the signs of misfortune in his domestic surroundings, and finally breaking into a fit of terror at the incident of the hated cat nestling beside him as he sleeps. The summoning of the servants and their vain attempts to put favorable interpretations on the incidents only confirm the deep superstitious faith of the poet in the impending sickness foretold by the feline intruder.

A later poem of the same collection, written during Ronsard's convalescence, gives an equally intimate picture of the poet. In *La Salade* we see Ronsard and his poet-secretary Amadys Jamyn setting out to gather greens and roots for their salad. While Ronsard looks about in fallow fields and solitary places, he instructs Jamyn:

Do thou go, Jamyn, another way,
And carefully seek out the lamb's lettuce
The little daisy with its tiny leaf,
The burnet wholesome for the blood,
And for the spleen, and for the aching side,
And I shall gather the companions of the moss,
The bell-flower with its sweet root,
And the bud of the tender goose-berries
Which are the first heralds of the Spring.

(La Salade, ll. 12-20)*

Then, returning to the prior's lodging at Croixval, they roll up their sleeves, wash the greens, add salt, rosé vinegar and olive oil from Provence. Turning to Jamyn, Ronsard continues, "Thou wilt say my fever tricks me, That I am mad, my salad and my Muse . . ." And Jamyn will be right, for Ronsard prefers his simple country life to the pompous pretensions of the court, where one must lie, flatter, and

[130]

disguise one's feelings. "To follow in the path of a Court/I am too sickly, too slothful, too deaf,/ Too fearful . . ." After a long digression on the vanity of earthly grandeur, the false glories of ambition, and the common end of it all–death–Ronsard returns to the praise of the simple rustic life of Vergil's peasant in the *Georgics* (IV, 125ff.) and reminds Jamyn that Hesiod and Horace have told us of the satisfactions of living close to nature, which is herself content with little, "But," says Ronsard, "I've preached enough. Give me my salad."

The other *poëmes* in these collections have titles which indicate that they are in some ways related to the *blason* of some favorite plant or animal: *Le Souci du jardin* (The Marigold), *Le Pin* (The Pine Tree), *Le Rossignol* (The Nightingale). They, too, in less obvious ways, show us something of Ronsard's private world. The nightingale, sitting in its juniper tree, reminds the poet and lover of his passionate affair with "Genèvre," a Parisienne whom he had met one evening on the banks of the Seine and for whom he composed some of his most sensual elegies and sonnets.[3] *Le Pin*, containing a moralization of the myth of Atys and Cybele, ends with these lines to a friend:

> Thus Cravan, I pass the day
> When fever, entrenched in my body
> Gnaws my bones, sucks my blood–thus
> The Muse can lighten care:
> Sickness can not sting us so that
> The pain grows not less by singing.

> (*Le Pin*, ll. 163-70)

Even the elaborate mythological poem *Hylas* is not without its personal touch. The poem, based on the medieval and Renaissance syntheses of various manifestations of Hercules and on the account (in the *Argonautica* and later classical poems) of the loss of his favorite page Hylas, contains like *Le Pin*, a moralization as well as narrative and descriptive passages. Here, as in so many of his appearances in Ronsard's poems, Hercules personifies the forces of civilization in combat against the primitive and barbaric elements which impede them. In choosing the story of Hercules' favorite Hylas, Ronsard exonerates the hero from the accusations of criminal behavior implied by ancient poets and portrays him as the teacher and guide of the handsome youth. Artistically, the scene at the fountain of the nymphs (who, overcome by Hylas' beauty, draw him beneath the waters) is among Ronsard's most exquisite descriptive passages. But the truly personal touch occurs at the end, when Ronsard, addressing his friend Jean Passerat, uses the ancient simile of the bee gathering pollen from the flowers and confides in him and in us the secret of his poetic composition:

> My Passerat, I resemble the bee
> Which gathers, now from the red flower,
> Now from the yellow; going from field to field
> She flies to the spot most pleasing to her,
> Laying in much food against the winter.
> Thus skimming and leafing through my books
> I gather, separate, and choose the finest,
> Which in a hundred hues I paint, now in one picture
> Now in another; and, master of my painting,
> Without constraint I imitate Nature.

> (*Hylas*, ll. 417-26)

The most personal, and in many ways the most touching, of the poems in the two books bears the simple title *A Cassandre*. Her name had not appeared in the poet's compositions for many years. Since her dazzling appearance at a court ball in 1545, Cassandre had become a matron and chatelaine, a neighbor of Ronsard's brother. Perhaps a chance meeting at La Possonnière had suddenly in a flood of memory brought back their youth. The result is one of Ronsard's finest poems, in which past and present blend, in which recollection is stronger than "reality," in which the idealization of the lady conquers the ravages of time:

> Not absence, forgetfulness, nor the day's swift course
> Have yet effaced the name, the grace, the love
> Which from my tender youth were printed in my heart,
> When I became the newest servant of Cassandra's beauty,
> Cassandra, much dearer to me than my eyes,
> Than my blood, my life, who only, everywhere,
> Was chosen by my Muse, for an everlasting theme
> That I might sing of thee in long-spun poesie.

Ronsard then recalls the stages of his obsession with the beauty and charm of the young Cassandre, how he became her captive, body and soul, so that her image has remained fixed within him till the very moment he sees her again. Then he continues:

> And if age, which breaks down fortresses and walls,
> Flowing on, has ravaged something of our youth,
> Cassandra, 'tis all the same! For I have no thought
> For what is present, but for the first glance,
> For the arrow, wounding me through thy childlike grace,
> Which still all bloody I feel within my breast.
> *(A Cassandre,* ll. 1-8; 23-28)

These few lines can only hint at the intense feeling which the original elegy conveys; nor can the translation echo the subtle harmony and music with which Ronsard surrounds this poetic conquest of time by affective memory.

II *Sonets pour Helene*

> Quand je devise assis aupres de vous,
> Tout le coeur me tressaut.
> Je tremble tout de nerfs & de genous,
> Et le pouls me defaut.
> Je n'ay ny sang ny esprit ny haleine,
> Qui ne se trouble en voyant mon Heleine,
> Ma chere & douce peine.
> *(Sonets pour Helene,* Livre I, vii)

Not long after writing the elegy to Cassandre, Ronsard, partially cured of his malarial fever, was summoned to court to contribute to a series of festivities which were planned to mark the conclusion of the Peace of Saint-Germain in 1570.[4] It was while he was in attendance at court composing poems for tourneys, royal *entrées,* and for other occasions, that Ronsard met the young lady whom he was to immortalize in his last sonnet sequence. The two books of *Sonets pour Helene,* first published in the collected edition of 1578, augmented and revised in 1584, have long been considered among the finest of Ronsard's poems. His vision of the experience of love has matured and, if he has lost some of the fire and vigor of the *Amours I* and the sweetness of *Amours II,* the new collection reveals the mastery of the sonnet sequence created in the poet's own distinctive style, a mastery we seek vainly in the earlier collections. For here Ronsard reveals fully that he is at last the equal of his greatest predecessors in the form.

In contrast to the earlier *Amours,* which were only gradually transformed by Ronsard to appear dedicated to a single lady, the poems to Hélène were from the beginning centered about the name and person of Hélène de Surgères, a young noblewoman in the celebrated "flying squadron" of ladies-in-waiting at the French court. She may have been introduced to Ronsard there or in the salon of the Maréchale de Retz, where a *précieux* society of courtiers and poets often gathered. Their friendship may have begun as a kind of courtly and playful banter. As the years passed Hélène, who was prudish and intellectual rather than passionate and sensual, took umbrage at the increasingly urgent desires of the aging poet. Like the *précieuses* of the following century satirized by Molière, she felt that physical love was demeaning; imbued with the Neoplatonic notions of Leon Hebreo, she sought love on a purely spiritual plane. For Ronsard this was a travesty of love and of nature. The diversity of their ages and temperaments led to quarrels and eventually to separation.

Though we know from Ronsard's contemporaries and from the other poets of the Retz salon a good deal more about the purely biographical aspects of Rondard's courtship of Hélène than we do about the earlier *Amours,* it is not easy to determine how much of the poetry is truly an account of the affair. To be sure, there are poems with specific settings—the stairs of the Louvre, a royal garden, Hélène dancing in an elaborate court ballet—just as there are mentions of dates, of festivals, and of the passing of months and years. This is really not important. It may be true that the name *Helen,* with all its associations with the legendary beauty of the Trojan war, first inspired Ronsard's interest. It may be equally true that the fairly numerous incidents which strike us as intimate details of the poet's courtship are perhaps only adaptations of themes found in the numerous minor Italian poets who were once again in vogue at court.[5] Or the incidents may actually have occurred in this refined society where nature often imitated art. In spite of all such hesitations we still have the impression that many of these poems reveal something of Ronsard's inner feelings about himself; they bear unmistakably the stamp of his distinct style; and they are personal in a way that distinguishes them from the earlier *Amours.*

For some time critics have thought that Ronsard was disturbed by the growing popularity of a fashionable young poet, Philippe Desportes, and that he had determined by composing a new sonnet sequence in the Italianate style to reassert his supremacy. Recent studies have questioned this supposition.[6] As for the strain of neo-Petrarchistic themes and conceits, the abstractions and conventions which are found both in the poems to Hélène and in those of Desportes, a reading of Ronsard's elegies and sonnets composed largely on commission in the 1560's will show that this fashion was not revived by Desportes, for it is already a prominent feature of these little-read poems. If this style, the direct predecessor of the *précieux* style, was revived among the courtiers and fashionable society of the time of Henri III, Ronsard may well share in the credit—or blame—for this mannered and "artificial" poetry. Dominant in the early collections of Desportes, in Ronsard's poems for Hélène it is only a secondary, and sometimes totally absent, feature.

This Italianate style is not, however, the chief attraction or interest of these poems for Hélène de Surgères. Rather the novelty of tone lies in the curious clash of traditional amorous themes and Ronsard's growing disillusionment with love as a mere *jeu de société,* a sophisticated game. Underneath the conventional compliments, the timeworn conceits of conquering eyes, Cupid's arrows, the sighs of the rebuffed lover, there appear the harsh realities of Ronsard's impatient sensuality, the ironic comments of the greying but experienced lover. It is these notes, quite absent from the usual sonnet sequence, which add the dissonance to the ordinarily cloying sweetness of such poems. The result is a new harmony, startling and complex.

In 1584 Ronsard added a number of sonnets, possibly intended originally for the collection but earlier published with *Amours Diverses.* A comparison of the two editions shows that Ronsard has become even bolder in expressing his sensual impatience and his disillusionment. There is, too, an unmistakable note of sadness, of irony, even of bitterness in many of these poems which increases the tension and enlarges the range of expression far beyond the conventional compliment. Hélène could not have been pleased. And yet "her" collection is among the finest sonnet sequences in any language.

In these poems Ronsard shows that his technique and command of his poetic instument has never been more masterful. Returning for most of the sonnets to the Alexandrine line abandoned during the composition of the *Franciade*, he uses all the devices learned from almost forty years as a writer of amorous verse and practitioner of the sonnet. Even such Petrarchan themes as the flight of the poet-lover from the crowded city and the observing gaze of friends to a solitary meditation take a new life and seem now a part of Ronsard's own experience:

> I flee the paths trodden by the boorish populace,
> And cities where people are heaped all together.
> The rocks, the forests are now full well aware
> What strange and solitary disposition marks my life.
>
> And yet I am not so alone, that Love my secretary
> Does not accompany my failing and feeble steps,
> That he does not recount my torments past and present
> To that voice [Echo] without body which can not hold her tongue.
>
> Often, full of fine words, to soothe my anguish,
> I stop and say: Could it really be true
> That she thinks of me, speaks, or remembers me?
>
> That my suffering begins to displease her pity?
> And though I may be wrong, deceived by the false,
> To please myself, Helene, I yet believe it true.
>
> (Livre I, xix, text of 1578)

Though readers of Horace and Petrarch will easily recognize Ronsard's debt to favorite authors, they will also notice the new note of self-mockery which adds another dimension to the poem. The flight from the *vulgus profanum*, the lover brooding alone, Love as keeper of secrets are all made personal and believable aspects of Ronsard's own life by the revelation of his self-deception and his own awareness of it.

This play of tension between desire and disappointment, between expectation and fulfillment, youth and age, and the feigned and the real binds many of the sonnets together. After all his protests to the reluctant and frigid young girl, Ronsard takes refuge in a dream world where fantasies are fulfilled, or else imagines the revenge of time upon the prudish beauty. In the world of dreams, at least, his desires can find contentment as they once did in his youthful *songes amoureux*. Here

are the opening lines of such a dream of love from the second book of
sonnets. I shall first cite the text in French to give the reader an
impression of the musical quality of the verse:

> Ces longues nuicts d'hyver, où la Lune ocieuse
> Tourne si lentement son char tout à l'entour,
> Où le Coq si tardif nous announce le jour,
> Où la nuict semble un an à l'ame soucieuse:
>
> Je fusse mort d'ennuy sans ta forme douteuse,
> Qui vient par une feinte alleger mon amour, . . .
>
> On those long winter nights when the langorous Moon
> So slowly turns her chariot in slow circles,
> When the late-rising Cock announces break of day,
> When the night seems a year to the care-filled soul:
>
> I should have died of grief but for thy wraith-like form
> Coming through a ruse to assuage my love, . . .
>
> (Livre II, xxiii)

After the strangely hallucinatory opening with its dreamy open vowels
and echoing hollow syllables Ronsard tells how the false image of
Hélène came to his bed to share his passion, spending the long winter
night in his arms, granting him in the world of fantasy the pleasures
denied him by the real Hélène. But he is only deceived for the moment;
the relief of frustrated desire brought to him by the phantom lady is
only acceptable because the reality is unattainable. The sonnet
concludes with an epigrammatic line tinged with bitter resignation: "To
trick oneself in love is not so bad a thing."

In the sonnet which directly follows this we have another fantasy,
this time projected into the future. In it Ronsard imagines himself
already dead, a "boneless fantom" enjoying the calm of the myrtle
grove in Hades, the special retreat of lovers; Hélène, still living but now
"an old woman crouching by the hearth" can only mumble the name of
her famous poet and regret her wasted youth, the roses she has failed to
pluck while they blossomed. In the context of the entire sequence, this
most famous sonnet, "Quand tu seras bien vieille, au soir'à la chandelle
. . .," takes on a note of irony and resignation scarcely hinted at in the
harmonies and cadences of the poem read in isolation.

Another wish-fantasy, removed from the sonnets in 1584 to the *Amours Diverses*, the *Chanson* "Plus estroit que la Vigne à l'Ormeau se marie . . .," is the poet's final orchestration of his invitation to follow Nature in the consummation of mutual love. For it Ronsard returns to the lyric form of his youthful odes, the four-line stanza of alternating Alexandrine and six-syllable lines; in it he creates one of the most melodious of his poems, in which the purely sensual opening is transcended by the vision of love which continues after death in the eternal spring of the Elysian Fields:

5

But sweetly suffering the yoke of thy rule
     However harsh it be
Into the Elysian Fields a single ship
     Will carry both of us.

6

There dead of too much love, beneath the myrtle bows
     Each day we'll see
The Heroes close by us together with their Heroines
     Speaking only of loves.

7

Now we shall dance beside the flowery strands
     To varied harmonies,
Now tired of the ball, we'll go beneath the shade
     Of laurels ever green: . . .

III *The Last Years*

After the publication of the great collected edition of his works in 1578, in which the *Sonets pour Helene* appeared for the first time, Ronsard withdrew more and more into a small circle of close friends. His visits to Paris and the court became rarer; when he was in the capital he was a guest of Jean Galland, who had succeeded his uncle as principal of the Collège de Boncourt. Ronsard's appearances at court were more or less "on command," for he still composed occasional poems for Henri III and, in spite of the fashionable success of Philippe Desportes, he was "poëte du roy." But as sickness and old age approached, Ronsard seems to have turned from the frivolous world of the courtiers toward an inner world of meditation on the great themes of poetry which he had encountered from the first in his reading of the ancient poets: the mutability of fortune, the vanity of human ambitions, the cycle of life and death. Had not these commonplaces of poetry been amply illustrated in the lives and deaths of his friends and his royal patrons, in his own career, and in the tragic events of the renewed civil and religious wars?

The repeated note of resignation before the passing of life, and with it of fame and glory, is characteristic of many of Ronsard's last poems. In an elegy—really an epistle in verse, like so many of his poems with this title—Ronsard addresses his young rival Desportes and sounds this very note of resignation. It is the voice of experience warning the younger poet of the vanity of literary, and indeed any, fame:

> We owe a debt to Death: both ourselves and our works;
> We die first of all, then age upon age unfolding
> Rolling onward swallows our work at last;
> This is the will of Nature and of mighty Destiny.
> God alone is eternal; of man's elements
> There remains after death not a vein or artery.
> Even worse, he feels, he reasons no more,
> A fleshless tenant of an ancient musty tomb.
>
> *(Elegie* à *Philippes Des-Portes,* 1584:
> ll. 1-8; Coh. II, 647; Laum. XVIII, 247)[7]

After a philosophical speculation on life and death, the body and the soul, Ronsard introduces two animal similes: the ox whose labor is rewarded meanly by wretched coarse food, and the ram whose wool warms the backs of ungrateful men. We poets, he tells Desportes, fare no better.

> As for me, I prefer thirty years of fame
> While I enjoy the Sun, to a thousand years
> After the hollow ditch has swallowed up my name
> And after our form has changed into another.
>
> (ll. 61-64)

So, Ronsard concludes, not without an ironic mention of Desportes' labors over Ariosto, the younger poet should enjoy pleasure while he can.

The theme of the transformation of matter, of life and death as an endless cycle, occurs several times in the poems of the last years. (One instance has just been cited in the passage above.) Of all the poems which treat this theme perhaps the most famous is the elegy first published in 1584 and subsequently (1623) entitled "Contre les bucherons de la forest de Gastine" (Against the Woodcutters of the Forest of Gastine). The occasion for the poem was the cutting down of large sections of the ancient forest near La Possonnière, the forest of which the Ronsards had been for generations the keepers for the lords of Vendôme. This forest, in which the young poet had wandered, where in his imagination he had glimpsed the forms of nymphs and sprites, was falling before the woodsman's ax. In the opening lines of the elegy Ronsard heaps curses on whoever touches these sacred trees (ll. 1-8), then he warns the woodcutter to hold back his ax and to realize that living forms inhabit the bark of the trees. I have translated two passages from this poem, a work rightly to be considered among the finest of Ronsard's and a summing up of so much of his most remarkable achievements. The first passage is Ronsard's farewell to the forest:

> Forest, lofty dwelling of the woodland birds,
> No more will the solitary stag and fleet hinds
> Feed peacefully beneath thy shade, and thy green mane
> No more will break the light of summer's sun.
> No more will the love-sick shepherd, leaning on a trunk,
> Blowing on his flute pieced with four holes,
> His sheep-dog at his feet, his crook by his side —
> No more recount his passion for his fair Jeanette;
> All will become silent; Echo will lose her voice,
> And thou become a field, in stead of thy woods,
> Whose unsure shadows slowly move,
> Wilt feel the plowshare, the cleaver, and the blade.
> Thy silence will be lost, and, panting with fright,
> No Satyrs nor Pans will come again to thee.
> Farewell, ancient forest, the plaything of Zephyr,
> Where first I learned to tune the tongues of my lyre,
> Where first I heard the singing arrows of
> Apollo, who came and struck my heart with awe.
> Where first, in amazement before the fair Calliope,
> I became a lover of the nine-fold band,
> When her hand cast scores of roses on my brow
> And with her very milk Euterpe suckled me.

Next Ronsard bids farewell to the great oaks of the forest, once the object of the countryman's veneration, now, bereft of leaves, the object of scorn. Thus ungrateful men slaughter the very oaks which in earliest times gave them sustenance. Then, considering the fate of this noble forest, Ronsard turns to a wider theme in the concluding lines of the elegy:

> How wretched is the man who trusts in this world!
> O Gods, how full of truth is that philosophy
> Which holds that everything will perish at the end,
> And, as it changes form will wear another one.
> The vale of Tempe will become one day a mountain
> And the peak of Athos a broad flat field,
> Neptune some day will be covered with wheat:
> Matter remains fast and its form is lost.

The poetic meditation inspired by the contemplation of the ancient forest and its iminent destruction is, in another poem, closely related in spirit and in form to the "méditations" of the Romantic poets.[8] The opening passage of the curious *Dialogue de Ronsard et des Muses delogées* finds the poet contemplating the clouds when he spies a flock of cranes flying, not in the traditional wedge but in square battle formation. These birds, he thinks, are leaving our cold land to return to the happier climate of their homes. Then he begins his meditation:

> As I watched their flight, I said to myself:
> I would, O birds, that I could do the same
> And see the fire flickering in my house,
> In my chimney, and never stir from there,
> Now that, ravaged by age, I have hair
> As grey as are your feathers.
> Farewell, winged flock, guests of Styrmion,
> Who, flying from Thrace to the Egyptians
> On the seashore, against the Pygmies
> Lead in light battle your feathery ranks.
> Return to your homes. Would I could as well.
> A man without a hearth is ever filled with care.
> But vainly I spoke to the squadron in flight,
> For the wind bore away, like it, my words
> As they filled with loud cries the encircling sky
> Happy to return to the place of their birth.

The principal subject of *Les Muses delogées,* however, is not the poet's meditation, which serves only as an introduction to the central allegory: the shameful neglect of the Muses by the new barbarians who now hold sway in France. But the bitterest denunciation of the courtiers of Henri III and the new barbarians is in a poem addressed to Ronsard's old friend and confidant, Simon Nicolas. No more scathing lines were written on the degenerate taste of the new age and its ignorant and vicious courtiers than are found in the *Caprice au seigneur Simon Nicolas*, published in the posthumous edition of 1587. The opening lines set the tone for the first part of the poem:

> All is lost, Nicholas, all grows worse;
> There is nothing left of the empire of France;
> Vice is reigning and virtue flies away;
> The great lords have adopted new pleasures,
> Mountebanks, clowns, wily courtiers
> Have now usurped the Muses' place,
> Gamesters, thieves, idlers, chatterboxes,
> Fops, astrologers, wranglers, swearers . . .

> (*Caprice* . . ., ll. 1-8; Coh. II, 675;
> Laum. XVIII, 315)

Now Ronsard almost regrets a lifetime spent in the service of the Muses, his struggles against ignorance and envy, which once again threaten to engulf France. Now, he admits, he is too old and feeble to take up the battle again. Perhaps, he thinks, some future poet may take his place and turn poetry away from the false taste of the new age. To this future successor Ronsard gives his last advice on poetry, a proud and final statement on learning, art, and glory. But war is at the gates, the king is childless, and Ronsard, appalled at the suffering and violence around him, utters a final prayer for Henri de Navarre who may save the land and one day bring in the dawn of a better day.

IV   Les Derniers Vers: *Ronsard's Last Poems*

To supervise the last collected edition of his works published during his lifetime Ronsard returned to Paris in 1584 and saw the great folio through the presses of Gabriel Buon. The court, which he now detested, received its official tribute in the peculiar section entitled "Bocage royal," a medley of earlier and more recent poems dedicated to royalty and to great patrons. Ronsard himself preferred the company of humanists, scholars, and young poets, whom he counselled in the gardens of his residence, the Collège de Boncourt. Among these younger men were his host Jean Galland and the young poet Claude Binet. To them we owe the preservation and publication of Ronsard's last verses, the splendid memorial service held in Boncourt chapel, the posthumous edition of Ronsard's works incorporating the poet's last revisions, and to Binet the first biography of the poet, containing a detailed account of Ronsard's last months.

His last sickness overtook Ronsard while he was a guest of Galland in Paris during the spring of 1585. In spite of inclement weather, the miserable roads, and the threat of civil war, Ronsard had a special litter constructed to ease the torture of moving his gout-ridden frame back to Touraine. By way of his priory at Saint-Giles de Montoire the party reached Croixval, where his condition grew worse. Even the opium, which he had begun taking some years before, failed to relieve his suffering. Wracked with pain and deprived of sleep, he longed for death. But he was not to meet death at Croixval. Undisciplined bands of Protestant looters were in the neighborhood, and Ronsard fled with his close friends and servants through the bitter cold of December to Saint-Cosme. There he prepared for death; he wrote his last will; he made his confession; he dictated from his deathbed his last poems; and, having bade farewell to his community, he died during the night of December 27–28, 1585.

In his *Derniers Vers* the poet has left a moving account of his last days. The stanzas, six sonnets, and two epitaphs contain the poet's cries of pain, his meditation on death, and his summary of his last moments. The first sonnet ("Je n'ay plus que les os, un squelette je semble . . .") is a grim self portrait of the emaciated sufferer, his body wasted by fever and pain, ". . . without flesh, nerves, muscles. . . ." In another sonnet he curses the long winter which seems endless to the insomniac. In still another he envies the lot of animals who can sleep through the misty winter cold without recourse to the poppy seeds and their failing qualities. Finally, as death approaches, he urges his soul to "pack its baggage" and prepare for the long journey to meet its Creator. But his real farewell is the sixth and final sonnet, "Il faut laisser maisons et vergers et jardins . . .:"   ·

We must leave houses and orchards and gardens
Vessels and plates engraved by the artisan
And sing our last rites, as does the swan
Who sings his death upon Meander's shores.

It is done, I have spun out the thread of my destiny,
I have lived, I have made my name right worthy,
My pen flies to Heaven to be a constellation
Far from worldly snares which trick the cleverest.

Happy the man who never was, happier he that returns
To nothing as he was, still happier the one that sojourns,
A man now made an angel close by Jesus Christ—

Leaving to rot below his outer form of mud
The plaything of Fate, of Fortune, and of Destiny—
Freed of the body's bonds and now etherial.

(Laum. XVIII, 180)

A study of the nature of the present one, a study of poetry rather than of the poet's place in the development of French literature, could find no more fitting conclusion than the lines composed by Ronsard for his own tomb. It is with them that I wish to close the book:

Pour son Tombeau

Ronsard repose icy, qui hardy dès enfance
Detourna d'Helicon les Muses en la France,
Suivant le son du Luth et les traits d'Apollon;
Mais peu valut sa Muse encontre l'éguillon
De la Mort, qui cruelle en ce tombeau l'enserre:
Son ame soit à Dieu, son corps soit à la terre.

(Coh. II, 637; Laum. XVIII, 181)

For His Tomb

Ronsard reposes here, who, bold from his youth on
Brought down from Helicon the Muses into France
Following the Lute's tones and Apollo's darts;
But scarce availed his Muse against the sting
Of cruel Death, who locks him in this tomb:
May his soul rest with God, his body with the earth.

CHAPTER 10

Conclusion

" O NE must regard Ronsard either as a charming country gentleman, or as a great historical figure in the development of French poetry, or as a poet; and the third aspect has a chance of being the most important." This is one of the few statements in J. Middleton Murray's essay on Ronsard (1919) with which one could presently agree. Too much is now known about Ronsard's life and its contingencies to regard him merely as a charming country gentleman, though to be sure there is some basis for this beguiling genre portrait. It is rather the history of Ronsard's influence on the subsequent development of French poetry which has particularly attracted scholars and critics. Thanks to their researches the history of this influence has been traced in some detail. Pervasive in France during Ronsard's lifetime, it remained so through the poetry of his disciples for several generations. Even with the radical changes in social and literary attitudes which rendered his poetry almost inaccessible to the Age of Louis XIV, we can not ignore the debt, however unacknowledged, which that period owed to the author who introduced in France the concept of the creative imitation of the Ancients. With the nineteenth century and the rediscovery of Ronsard, the story becomes more complicated; for that reason, perhaps, less attention has been given to this later period. In any case the emphasis on historical development has tended to blur the focus on the poetry itself and has led a number of critics to commit the sin which, in the eyes of the historian Lucien Febvre, is unforgivable: anachronism.

"Each era," says Febvre, "fashions in its mind its own universe. . . . Similarly, each era fashions in its mind its representation of the historical past." These observations are true not only of the historical past, but of figures in that.past. Thus with Ronsard each generation has found its own poet by taking that part of the legend or of the poems which most harmonized with its own desires and aspirations: the Ronsard of the Romantics, a lover of nature and a superb lyrist for Sainte-Beuve, a prophetic seer for Victor Hugo; the Parnassian master of forms, of rhymes and rhythms, for Théodore de Banville; the languid *fin de siècle* esthete for Walter Pater; the swashbuckling, lusty, militant Catholic for an ultra Tory like Wyndham Lewis; and, more recently, the star-haunted poet brooding over the universe, or the baroque stylist of unexpected originality. And, surviving all these fashions with a remarkable tenacity, the Ronsard of the anthologies—the light lyrist, easy, graceful, charming, but really quite superficial.

Each of these partial versions may contain a portion of the whole poetry of Ronsard, but each alone is a distortion. For the entire body of that poetry is as varied, as rich, and as full of movement and color as the age in which it was written and sung. And it is, perhaps, the most comprehensive expression of the French Renaissance we have. In this poetry are found the earthy sensuality and wit of Rabelais together with his humanistic aspirations, the new learning, scenes of court and countryside, of battle and conflict, religious and political invective and dispute, satire, songs for festivals and pageants, amorous ditties, philosophical and scientific speculation, obsessions of desire and death, and finally,—nourished at the same sources of the Ancients and of experience,—the wisdom of Montaigne. Some of this great poetic universe appears barren and monotonous, for we have largely lost the taste to savor the artifices enjoyed by a Renaissance audience. Other portions seem at first forbidding, since they do not appear to offer immediate rewards. But much still remains that offers to those who delight in poetry the pleasures which only the Muse can grant.

How, finally, shall one assess this vast achievement? By what has been, historically, important in the development of French literature? By what is today fashionable in terms of poetic value, or deemed worthy of scrutiny by critics? Perhaps Ronsard's avowed goal may give us a clue: not to found a school of poetry, not to swell the French language by large doses of foreign or archaic words, not to ape slavishly Greek, Latin, or Italian authors, not to fix literary genres or poetic forms, but to imitate Nature, called the Cosmos because of the beauty of her infinite variety. With his ardent temperament, considerable learning, unsparing labors, sure intelligence, and subtle ear for the melodies of his own language he succeeded in no small measure.

Notes and References

1. Most biographies follow the dates established in P. Laumonier's critical edition of Binet's *Vie de Pierre de Ronsard*. All dates given here are adapted to the modern calendar. More detailed chronologies may be found in Chamard, *Histoire de la Pléiade* vol. IV; R. Lèbegue, *Ronsard, l'homme et l'oeuvre;* and P. Gadoffre, *Ronsard par lui-même*.

See for early years M. Dassonville, *Ronsard. Étude historique et littéraire. I. Les Enfances Ronsard.* This work appeared after the present study was already complete.

Chapter One

1. Pierre de Ronsard, *OEuvres complètes,* ed. Paul Laumonier; completed by Raymond Lebègue and Isidore Silver (Paris, 1914–68), 18 vols. This is the great critical edition to which most references in the text refer. Hereafter abbreviated as Laum.

2. Pierre de Ronsard, *OEuvres complètes*, ed. Gustave Cohen (Paris: Gallimard), 2 vols. Text of 1584. Hereafter referred to as Coh. For a listing of the reprints of other editions of Ronsard's text see the section on Ronsard in Cabeen's *A Critical Bibliography of French Literature*, vol. II. To this list should be added the text of 1587 presently being published in an edition prepared by Professor Silver (University of Chicago and Didier), of which four volumes have appeared.

3. Little attention has been paid in this study to the posthumous history of Ronsard's fame and influence. Attention is focused rather on the poetry itself and on the aspects of Ronsard's life and times that help to elucidate it.

4. The recent tendency of Ronsard scholars to belittle or ignore the accomplishments of their predecessors seems unfortunate. The attitude expressed by Professor Steele Commager in his preface to his study of *The Odes of Horace* (Yale University Press, 1962; Indiana University Press, 1967) seems more appropriate: "Since we have inevitably to stand upon the shoulders of previous scholars, it ill becomes us to step on their toes in getting there."

5. Frances A. Yates, *The French Academies of the Sixteenth Century* (London, 1947), p. 151.

6. Jean Seznec, *The Survival of the Pagan Gods* (New York, 1953), p. 309.

7. In addition to the book by Miss Yates (note 5 above) one should consult the valuable comments of G. Gadoffre (*Ronsard par lui-même*) on the importance of the humanist movements in the formation of Ronsard and his friends.

Chapter Two

1. A detailed description of the manor house and the surrounding country,

together with an anthology of Ronsard's poems mentioning them, may be found in P. Laumonier, *Ronsard et sa province* (Paris, 1924).

2. See Pierre Champion, *Ronsard et son temps* (Paris, 1925), pp. 27-30.

3. I here follow the opinion of H. Weber in his valuable study *La Création Poètique au XVIe siècle en France* (Paris, 1956), 2 vols. (I, 71-79); and G. Gadoffre, *Ronsard par lui-même,* pp. 12-16.

4. Detailed information on Dorat may be found in Pierre de Nolhac, *Ronsard et l'humanisme* (Paris, 1921 and 1966), a remarkable study of the humanistic movement. The recent reprinting of the original book shows how little this work has dated. Additional, and more recent, information on Ronsard's studies in Greek and his proficiency in that language may be found in I. Silver's *Ronsard and the Hellenic Renaissance in France* (St. Louis, 1961), vol. I chs. 2-4.

5. G. Gadoffre, "L'Université collégiale et la Pléiade," *French Studies,* XI (1957), 293-304.

6. The text of Baïf's "Le Papillon" is in Laum. VI, 97-101. It is cited as well in I. Silver's *Ronsard and the Hellenic Renaissance,* I, 46.

7. The complete text is in Laum. III, 184-217; Coh. 454-64.

Chapter Three

1. There is a much more detailed treatment of "nature" and "imitation" in Grahame Castor, *Pléiade Poetics* (Cambridge University Press, 1964), pp. 54ff. I have avoided the discussion of the ambiguities in Ronsard's use of "nature" and "truth" and his apparently puzzling statement that the poet's task is to imitate nature through such guides as Homer. Ronsard's practice of poetry is often superior to the expression of his poetic theories.

2. H. Weber, *La Création poétique* . . ., I, 116-17, says: "The only true originality of the Pléiade lies in their refusal to imitate the French poets who preceded them and their unique adherence to the Ancients and the Italians." Weber's entire chapter on "Les Theories poétiques" (I, 107-60) is well worth reading.

3. Critics have been almost unanimous in recognizing that Ronsard's superior gifts and his own intense feeling for the concrete, portrayed in movement, enabled him to exploit and to transcend the theories and conventions of his time.

4. Translation:

> Mouldy with time thy wood gave forth no sound;
> Then I was moved with pity for thy sad state,
> Thou who once made the feasts of great kings
> More succulent and sweet.
> To restore thy strings and thy frame
> And specially a tone natural to thee,
> I pillaged Thebes and sacked Appulia,
> Making thee rich with their fine spoils.

5. Translation:

> I wish to build thee an ode
> Fashioning it in the style
> Of thy honored palaces
> Which frequently have their entry
> Decorated with great marbles
> And with lofty gilt pillars.

6. See Vianey's discussion of imitation and freedom in *Les Odes de Ronsard* (Paris, 1932ff.), pp. 28ff. Vianey stresses the original, French qualities of the odes of 1550.

7. This is the opinion of P. Laumonier, *Ronsard, poète lyrique* (Paris, 1923), his monumental study of the history and sources of Ronsard's poetry in stanza form. There he gives a survey of the history of the ode and the *chanson*, together with a discussion of possible Italian and neo-Latin influences. A more recent study is found in Carol Maddison, *Apollo and the Nine: A History of the Ode* (Baltimore, 1960); pp. 226-75 deal specifically with Ronsard and the French ode.

8. Gustave Cohen, *Ronsard, sa vie et son oeuvre* (Paris, 1923ff.), p. 93. Other comments by Cohen show a sympathetic reading, but he tends to condemn whatever departs from his ideal, Victor Hugo.

It is notable that, until quite recently, critics, while mentioning the musical setting of the odes, have tended to ignore the capital role of the music in relation to the structure and tonal effects of the text.

9. For several of these comments I am indebted to C. M. Bowra, *Pindar* (Oxford, 1964), in particular pp. 4-41; 170ff.

10. Laum. I, 90-98; Coh. I, 378-82.

11. Translation:

> I shall, still living, fly through the world
> Making eternal the fields where I dwell,
> Covered and made fertile with my fame;
> Thus by my joining the two divers harpers [Pindar and Horace]
> To the sweet prattling of my ivory lyre
> They recognize themselves in my verses of Vendôme.

12. Some of the opinions expressed in the preceding pages are a result not only of a rereading of the text of Horace, but of two studies of his poetry: Jacques Perret, *Horace* (New York, 1964) and Steele Commager, *The Odes of Horace* (New Haven, 1962). I wish to acknowledge a special debt to Professor Commager's book.

13. John C. Lapp, "The Potter and His Clay: Mythological Imagery in Ronsard" in *The Classical Line. Essays in Honor of Henri Peyre* (Yale French Studies, 38; 1967), pp. 93ff.

14. The best account of this gradual reconciliation is found in the masterful study of Marcel Raymond, *L'Influence de Ronsard sur la poésie française (1550-1585)*, (Paris, 1927; Geneva, 1966). As Raymond notes, there was really no "school of Marot," but rather isolated poets who still followed Marot's style. The advice of Ronsard's protectors and the lack of agreement among his critics may explain the possibility of compromise reached by the old and the new poets.

Chapter Four

1. An elaborate study of Ronsard's love poetry is found in the three volumes of Fernand Desonay's *Ronsard, poète de l'amour* (Brussels, 1953-59). This study contains not only a summary of most important opinions on Ronsard's amorous verse and the women who may have inspired it, but Professor Desonay's own stimulating comments on these collections, together with documentation concerning their musical settings.

2. Desonay, III, 166-75. In addition to the arguments of Sorg, Desonay notes the numerous echos of Petrarch in the poems on the death of Marie. Here is his conclusion (p. 175); "All this leads us to believe that the pieces *Sur la Mort de Marie* have very little connection with the Angevine girl from Bourgueil. . . ."

3. See Donald Stone, Jr., *Ronsard's Sonnet Cycles* (New Haven, 1966), p. 9. "Ronsard undoubtedly may have fallen in love during his lifetime, but these poems witness that he rarely if ever chose to write of love without the awareness that he was writing poetry."

4. Throughout this chapter, as well as in the discussion of the *Sonnets pour Hélène*, I have also referred to the useful edition of Ronsard's love poems by H. and C. Weber: Ronsard, *Les Amours* (Paris, 1963).

5. Stone emphasizes the element of conventional complement in *Amours I* and finds the sensual element subordinate to it. My own opinion is in agreement with M. Desonay (*Ronsard, poète de l'amour*, I) and is confirmed in a recent review of Stone's book by H. Weber. This difference of opinion in no way implies lack of appreciation for the insights into Ronsard's poetry offered in Mr. Stone's book.

6. Both Desonay and Weber have given elaborate evidence to show that the subsequent revisions of *Amours I* by Ronsard tended, in general, to break the impulsive rhythm (of which Desonay makes a number of analyses) and to soften the "baroque" effects of images, repetition, and so on. The sensuality is thus often eliminated or considerably attenuated in the later texts.

7. See Stone, pp. 90-91.

8. Stone observes (p. 52): "The concept of a sonnet cycle has clearly been lost."

9. Translation of the text of 1555:

> Soft, fair, gentle, and sweet-smelling Rose,
> How rightly to Venus thou art consecrated!
> Thy delicate scent gives new life to men and gods.
> In short, Rose, thou art fair above all things.
> Grace, for her head, composes a chaplet
> Of thy leaf, and ever her breast with it is dressed.
> A thousand times a day does gay Cytherea,
> For her rouge, sprinkle with thy dew her fair cheek.
> By Zeus, how pleased I am when I see thee
> Blossom at daybreak on some hidden stem
> Within some garden near a solitary wood.
> Of thee are formed the breast and arms of Nymphs,
> From thee the Dawn derives her cheek and hand,
> And her complexion she who is the mother of Love.

Chapter Five

1. J. Vianey, in *Les Odes de Ronsard* (Paris, 1932), gives examples of all these revisions and a detailed study of the variants of several short odes, pp. 122-44. In general Vianey's comments on the revisions show him in favor of the later versions. See also on this subject of revisions I. Silver, "Deux points de vue sur Ronsard 'aristarque de ses oeuvres' " *Revue d'Histoire littéraire de France*, LVIII, 1-15.

2. P. Laumonier, *Ronsard, poète lyrique*, 2nd ed. (Paris, 1923), is still the authoritative work on the history and development of Ronsard's poetry in lyric form. Additional information on the poems inspired by the Greek Anthology may be found in James Hutton's "Ronsard and the Greek Anthology," *Studies in Philology*, LX, 103-27. C. Maddison gives a full list of Anacreontic poems used by Ronsard in *Apollo and the Nine*, p. 269.

3. His professed indifference to older historical scholarship has led G. Gadoffre (*Ronsard par lui-même*, p. 50) to make erroneous comments of this sort in an otherwise excellent study of Ronsard. Speaking of this poem he says: "At the age of thirty-eight [*sic*] he is already a toothless old man complaining of bad digestion, bad circulation, insomnia and fever. At no time does he attempt a flattering self-portrait." Then he quotes the first stanza of Ronsard's adaptation of the Greek poem. The real self-portraits of Ronsard are found in the poems of 1560 and after.

4. The text of Sappho may be found in *Lyra Graeca*, ed. J. M. Edwards (Loeb Classical Library), I, 186-87. There is an excellent French version with commentary in Henri Bonnard's *Civilisation grecque*, 3 vols. (Lausanne, 1954-59), I, 96. (An English translation of Bonnard is also available.) The Catullus poem is No. LI, "Ille mi par deo videtur . . ."

5. A recent study of the *blason* in English may be found in D. B. Wilson, *Descriptive Poetry in France from Blason to Baroque* (Manchester, 1967). Particular attention is given the anatomical *blason* on pp. 15ff. For Ronsard's *blasons*, pp. 57-67. A scholarly examination of the animal *blasons* will be found in H. Naïs, *Les Animaux dans la Poésie française de la Renaissance* (Paris, 1961).

6. Translation:

> As soon as thou art sprinkled
> At break of day, with dew,
> Thy thousand speeches fill the air:
> With thy wings the air's a-flutter,
> And, hanging in the sky, with thy chatter
> Thou tellest thy loves to the winds.

(Laum. VI, 246)

Chapter Six

1. I have given only the slightest notion of the history and development of Ronsard's hymns. For more information the reader may consult H. Chamard, *Histoire de la Pléiade*, 4 vols. (Paris, 1939; 1961), vol. II; the introduction to Laumonier's ed. (vol. VIII). M. Dassonville, "Eléments pour une définition de l'hymne ronsardien," *Bibliothèque d'Humanisme et Renaissance*, XXIV, 58-76, re-examines Ronsard's concept of the *hymne* in view of his entire work in this genre. Professor Dassonville is at present engaged in a book-length study of this neglected aspect of Ronsard's poetry.

2. P. Laumonier's notes frequently emphasize Ronsard's deletion of dedications to members of this family in the editions of 1567ff. What is remarkable is that so many dedications of major poems are, in fact, retained in these editions. In some cases the revision of the text actually introduces the name "Odet" lacking in earlier versions. The fact that the entire family had become leaders in

the Protestant cause and that both the admiral and the cardinal had died before 1578 underscores Ronsard's devotion to their memory and indicates the sincerity of his feelings toward them.

3. In a study of this scope I have not felt it possible to examine in any detail the themes of the hymns and their recurrence in the two books. They will doubtless receive the attention of Professor Dassonville in his forthcoming study of these poems.

4. J. Frappier, "L'Inspiration biblique et théologique de Ronsard dans l'Hymne de la Justice," in *Mélanges d'histoire littéraire de la renaissance offerts à Henri Chamard* (Paris, 1951), 97-108 and "Tradition et Actualité dans 'l'Hymne de l'Or' de Pierre de Ronsard" in *Literary History & Literary Criticism* (New York, 1965), 126-41, shows the connection between the person to whom the hymn is dedicated, the events associated with his life, and the themes of the poems. M. Dassonville in the study mentioned in note 1. above also points to these connections.

5. Much of Ronsard's poetry for royalty and the great noble families is, in a sense, official; as such it follows the tradition of such poetry in emphasizing the virtues and finer qualities of the subject of the poem. In the case of eulogies and epitaphs this is especially obvious.

6. See my comment in note 2 above.

7. A curious passage, in autobiographical form, related to the infernal chase has been omitted from later versions of the *Hymne des Daemons*, in my opinion a regrettable omission.

8. A thorough and informative treatment of the ancient hymn and its development through the Alexandrian period may be found in the article "Hymnos" in the Paulys-Wissowa *Realencyclopädie der Classischen Altertumswissenschaft*, XI, pt. 1, 142-83. See especially pp. 143-69.

9. For this aspect of Ronsard's world see André-Marie Schmidt, *La Poésie scientifique en France au XVIe siècle* (Paris, 1940), pp. 92-99. A more recent study in English will be found in D. B. Wilson, *Ronsard, Poet of Nature* (Manchester, 1961), pp. 1-8; 61-75. Wilson's views are sometimes in opposition to those of Schmidt, Gadoffre, Frappier, and Dassonville.

10. Studies, in English, of the *Hymne de l'Automne* will be found in Donald Stone, *Ronsard's Sonnet Cycles* and D. B. Wilson, *Ronsard, Poet of Nature*.

Chapter Seven

1. The dual aspect of Ronsard's role as court poet is studied by I. Silver in his article "Pierre de Ronsard: Panegyrist, Pensioner and Satirist of the French Court," *Romanic Review*, XLV, 89-108.

2. Since Ronsard's probable sources, both Graeco-Latin and biblical, use much the same vocabulary and imagery (i.e., turning swords into plowshares), it is difficult to be sure whether he is consciously following any one author, or has retained these images from his reading of all of them.

3. These pacifist sentiments are likely as "sincere" (or perhaps more so) as Ronsard's bravura passages celebrating feats of arms. One would expect a member of the nobility, brought up to bear arms, to praise the martial abilities of the great. The denunciation of the futilities of dynastic strife, expression of compassion for the sufferings of the innocent, and indignation at the senseless

slaughter of troops are certainly less to be expected from a writer of Ronsard's class and time. They are another evidence of the deep imprint of humanistic studies and values on this descendant of feudal warriors.

4. Many Renaissance treatises on government have common sources in antiquity, a fact which may partially explain the similarity of concept, substance, and expression in many of them. In view of this, it is not surprising to find similarities in the Latin poems of Dorat and L'Hospital and the French poems of du Bellay and Ronsard written for the instruction of François II and Charles IX. I hope to examine these relationships in a separate study.

5. Du Bellay had died during the night of January 1, 1560. This passage is one of the rare mentions of Ronsard's former classmate in his poetry following du Bellay's death.

6. French critics, with their tradition of classical rhetoric, almost unanimously condemn the use of personification or allegory. An example among many may be cited from Professor Lebègue's survey, *La Poésie française de 1560 à 1630* (Paris, 1951), I, 30, where he says of the figure Opinion' "This cold allegory, in conformity with the taste of the time, appears to us quite tiresome." I do not mean to imply that we should undiscriminatingly accept whatever is "of the time." I do, however, think it is important to realize how widely accepted such allegorical personifications were, and how much a part of the public festivities and entertainments of the age they appear to have been.

7. This personification of France bears a strikingly close resemblance to the figure drawn in a patriotic prose work by Alain Chartier, the *Quadrilogue invectif* likewise addressed to the "four estates," written toward the close of the Hundred Years War.

8. Like many Catholics of his time Ronsard failed to distinguish between the zeal inspired by the religious convictions of devout Protestants and the fanaticism and brutality which hid behind it in those who, for selfish reasons, attached themselves to this party. As the wars flared up again and again, he was, like Montaigne, clearly aware that a large number on both sides were using religion as a cloak to cover private ambitions.

9. This ancient image of the poet making his verses like the bee gathering its nectar is Ronsard's most felicitous expression of his practice of "innutrition," i.e., of absorbing and converting the poetry of the ancients by the blending of images and themes with his own substance to form a new poem.

Chapter Eight

1. Ronsard composed five sonnets on the occasion of the visit of Charles IX, the Queen Mother, and the king's younger brother, later Henri III (Laum. XIV, 121-25). One senses the hyperbole common to such occasions, but also, on the part of Ronsard, a real devotion to the young monarch and a sense of satisfaction in his newly bestowed priory.

2. See Chapter 4, note 2.

3. Also composed as an epilogue to a play presented at Fontainebleau as part of the same entertainments is the poem which begins: "Ici la Comedie apparoist un example . . ." (Laum. XIV, 212-14), sometimes reprinted in anthologies. Here is a translation of the opening lines:

Here the Play appears as an example
In which each beholds the truth of his deeds:
The world is the Theatre, and men the actors.
Fortune, who is mistress of the Scene,
Prepares the costumes, and of the life of man
The heavens and fates are the lofty spectators.

4. There is still some disagreement over whether the *Bergerie* was actually presented at court or not. The opposing points of view may be examined in P. Laumonier's introduction to the critical edition (vol. XIII) and in H. Chamard, *Histoire de la Pléiade.*

5. E. Bourciez, *Les Moeurs polies et la littérature de cour sous Henri II* (Paris, 1888), p. 212. See also H. Chamard, *Histoire de la Pléiade,* III, 97ff.

6. All critics are more or less in agreement in finding these faults in the poem. The reader interested in a more detailed account may consult, in addition to the section of Chamard mentioned in note 5, Laumonier's introduction to vol. XVI.

7. In his article "Ronsard, poète officiel," *Studi in onore di V. Lugli e D. Valeri* (Venice, 1961), II, 573-87, Professor Lebègue adds further observations to the study by I. Silver on Ronsard's role as a court poet, mentioning particularly the didactic intention of the historical account of the reign of the "Rois fénéants."

Chapter Nine

1. Another *hymne-blason*, the curious and fanciful poem entitled "L'Ombre du cheval" (The Horse's Shadow), is conjectured by P. Laumonier to be the imaginary portrait of a gift promised by Belot to Ronsard but not delivered. It is thus a reminder to the forgetful patron that the poet is still waiting for his horse.

2. This opening passage has led some students of Ronsard's philosophical poetry to see in his later work a tendency to an Averroistic view of the universe, a tendency which he curbs by careful qualifications showing that the human soul is distinct from the world and that it is guided directly by God.

3. These poems have been reprinted in the edition of Ronsard's love poems published by H. and C. Weber (*Les Amours* [Paris, 1963]) and are among the collections studied by Desonay and Stone.

4. For Ronsard's collaboration with Dorat in arranging the decorations and inscriptions for arches, and the recitation of poems, for the royal progresses, see Laum. XV, pp. 389ff.

5. See particularly F. Desonay, *Ronsard, Poète de l'amour*, II, 264-66. The entire discussion in Desonay concerning this sonnet sequence is well worth reading and goes far toward dispelling the sentimental biographical readings of certain of the poems taken out of context.

6. The complex problem of the mutual influences of Ronsard and Desportes is the subject of two studies in the *Biblothèque d'Humanisme et Renaissance*, vol. XXVIII: Mary Morrison, "Ronsard and Desportes" (pp. 294-322); and Claude Faisant, "Les Relations de Ronsard et Desportes" (pp. 323-53). My own reading of the neglected Ronsard poems of the 1560's had led me to a conclusion similar to M. Faisant's (p. 332).

7. The text of the poems cited in the remainder of this chapter is taken from G. Cohen's edition *(Biblothèque de la Pléiade).* The final volume of text in the critical edition (vol. XVIII) has just appeared and may now be consulted.

8. See H. Naïs, *Les Animaux dans la poésie française de la Renaissance* (Paris, 1961), pp. 407-8.

Selected Bibliography

(See the Chronology for the principal works and collected editions published by Ronsard during his lifetime.)

PRIMARY SOURCES

PIERRE DE RONSARD. *Les Amours,* ed. H. and C. Weber. Paris: Garnier, 1963. Complete edition of love poems in one volume. The text follows the principles of the critical edition, with selection of variants, useful notes, and glossary.

———. *OEuvres Choisies,* ed. Pierre de Nolhac. Paris: Garnier, 1966 (reprint). Best available anthology, with good selection from entire works. Text of various editions. Limited notes and glossary.

———. *OEuvres complètes,* ed. Gustave Cohen. Paris: Gallimard, 1938, 2 vols. Text of 1584, with selected variants and notes. Useful edition, but misleading without control of critical edition.

———. *OEuvres complètes,* ed. Paul Laumonier; completed by Raymond Lebègue and Isidore Silver. Paris: Didier, 1914-1968, 18 vols. The great critical edition, producing the text of Ronsard's first published version and all variants through 1587. Indispensable for serious reader.

Lyrics of Ronsard, translated by W. Stirling. London: Allan Wingate, 1956. French text facing verse translations, chosen mainly from light lyrics.

SECONDARY SOURCES

BISHOP, MORRIS. *Ronsard, Prince of Poets.* Oxford University Press, 1940; Michigan University Press, 1964. Easy style, interesting on background; dated, biographical reading of love poems; good verse translations.

DESONAY, FERNAND. *Ronsard, poète de l'amour.* Brussels: Palais des Académies, 1952-59. 3 vols. Thorough, scholarly, original treatment of entire body of love poems.

GADOFFRE, GILBERT. *Ronsard par lui-même.* Paris: Editions du Seuil, 1960. Stimulating introduction to facets of poet often ignored; selection of lesser known passages from works.

LAUMONIER, PAUL. *Ronsard, poète lyrique.* Paris: Hachette, 1923. 2nd. ed. Still a masterful historical treatment of the subject, though some evaluations subject to revision.

LEBÈGUE, RAYMOND. *Ronsard, l'homme et l'oeuvre.* Paris: Hattier-Boivin, 1950. Succinct introduction; examination of principal collections.

NOLHAC, PIERRE DE. *Ronsard et l'humanisme.* Paris: Champion, 1921. Unsurpassed for intellectual formation of Ronsard.

RAYMOND, MARCEL. *Baroque et Renaissance poétique. Ronsard et Malherbe.* Paris: José Corti, 1954. Appraisal of aspects of Ronsard in relation to the baroque.

STONE, DONALD, JR. *Ronsard's Sonnet Cycles.* New Haven: Yale University Press, 1966. A new examination of the cycles, based on "tone and vision" rather than style; corrects traditional conceptions.

WEBER, HENRI. *La Création poétique au XVIe siècle en France.* Paris: Nizet, 1956. 2 vols. Explications of Ronsard poems in vol. I are masterful.

WILSON, D. B. *Ronsard Poet of Nature.* Manchester University Press, 1961. Good for background on an important aspect of Ronsard's poetry.

The following studies have appeared since the text of the present study was completed and have not been incorporated into opinions expressed:

ARMSTRONG, ELIZABETH. *Ronsard and the Age of Gold.* Cambridge: Cambridge University Press, 1968.

DASSONVILLE, MICHEL. *Ronsard. Etude historique et littéraire. I. Les enfances Ronsard.* Geneva: Drox, 1968.

SILVER, ISIDORE. *The Intellectual Evolution of Ronsard. I. The Formative Influences.* St. Louis: Washington University Press, 1969

TERREUX, L. *Les Poèmes de Ronsard antérieurs à 1560: Etude et Interprétation des variantes.* Geneva: Droz, 1968.

Index